THE ATLANTIC LITERARY REVIEW

Quarterly

A Peer Reviewed Journal Indexed in
MLA Directory of Periodicals

JULY – SEPTEMBER 2015

VOLUME 16 NUMBER 3

ATLANTIC
PUBLISHERS & DISTRIBUTORS (P) LTD

CONTRIBUTORS

Mahima Singh, Guest Lecturer, DAV PG College, Varanasi.

Aindrilla Guin, Assistant Professor of English, Bankura University, Bankura, West Bengal.

Reena Mitra, Professor in English, Amity School of Languages, Amity University, Lucknow, Uttar Pradesh.

Tapu Biswas, Assistant Professor, Department of English, Visva-Bharati, Santiniketan.

Roger Augustine, St Joseph's College for Women, Gorakhpur.

Shahaji V. Gaikwad, Associate Professor and Head, Department of English, M.S.S. Arts, Commerce and Science College, Jalna.

Sharmistha Chatterjee (Sriwastav), Assistant Professor, Department of English, Alih University, Kolkata.

Smita Jha, Associate Professor, Department of Humanities & Social Sciences, IIT, Roorkee.

Mukunda Upadhyaya, Associate Professor, Department of English, Chaiduar College, Gohpur, Assam, Gauhati University.

Radhakant Mishra, Retired Reader in English, Mahalaxmi Nagar, Bolangir, Odisha.

Amrita Satapathy, PhD Assistant Professor School of Humanities, Social Sciences & Management Indian Institute of Technology, Bhubaneswar, Odisha.

THE ATLANTIC LITERARY REVIEW
VOLUME 16 NUMBER 3 (JULY-SEPTEMBER 2015)

TABLE OF CONTENTS

Text vs. Screen: Jhumpa Lahiri's *The Namesake*

Mahima Singh

Film is a dynamic process of technological representation that makes alive the imagination and feelings of writer who writes from his/her own consciousness. But the film is not mere projection of textual values rather goes beyond as filmmakers employ their imaginative faculties to recreate the events of novel on celluloid screen. Film and fiction are two different art forms: they differ from each other in terms of structure, perception, narrative and in many other ways. The transformation of literary space into visual space allows free flow of imagination that may reproduce the given realities of the text into the imaginative possibilities of different space. This space is more creative because differences between movie and novel can be marginalized and maximized as a filmmaker sometimes makes some cuts and sometimes interpolates scenes and characters. Visual imagination offers a wide range of scope for cognitive faculties than reading and directly appeals to the human senses by bringing out human feelings, emotions and sentiments through lights, colour, camera, action, sound, dialogues and characters.

Jhumpa Lahiri's *The Namesake* (2003) represents the limited space of Bengali immigrant in America which is a world without an axis, easily collapsible, deceptive, where the state of exile is cultural as well as emotional. She depicts conflict between two different cultures, two generations—one that has migrated and the other who has born there with bicultural identity and experiences a tormenting ambivalence towards the adopted lifestyle and inherited culture. Mira Nair has transposed Lahiri's *The Namesake* into visual poetics on celluloid in 2007. Like Lahiri, she portrays life of diasporic people with their quest for identity, generation difference between Gogol and his immigrant parents and irreconcilable cultures of East and West. Nair's adaptation is not only expression of Lahiri's ideas into different medium rather a re-creation and radicalization of ideology through her visual venture. She has successfully turned

Lahiri's elusive narration into motion picture and focused on poignant feelings of immigrant experiences.

The novel begins with newly-wedded Bengali couple Ashima and Ashok Ganguli who have migrated to America and expecting their first baby Gogol in a foreign land and after some years Sonia is born. Ashima suffers from loneliness and pain of becoming a mother in a foreign land. She is full of terror of raising children in a country where she knows no one. Lahiri portrays cultural displacement and emigrated experiences of them in their adopted homeland which is only oscillation between fact and fantasy, tradition and modernity and in their past and present. She richly explicates diasporic existence where characters are involved in two cultures simultaneously. *The Namesake* focuses on the hyphenated identities of Indian-Americans; chiefly it deals with the identity dilemma of Gogol Ganguli and his rebel against his odd nomenclature. He is named after his father's favorite Russian author Nikolai Gogol. As Gogol grows up in the American culture, he realizes that his identity is an imposed one. He thinks that the Russian name leads him neither American nor Indian, rather merely irrelevant and ludicrous, lacking in dignity and gravity. Throughout the novel, he is haunted by his strange name, he wonders about the reason for having such an unusual name. But his father has no doubt about the appropriateness of the name. To him, Gogol was his savior when terrible train accident took place, he was almost left by search party but he had been saved in last moment. He remembers it:

> But the lantern's light lingered, just long enough for Ashok to raise his hand, a gesture that he believed would consume the small fragrant of life left in him. He was still clutching a single page of *The Overcoat* crumpled tightly in his fist, and when he raised his hand the wad of paper dropped from his fingers. "Wait!" he heard a voice cry out. "The fellow by the book. I saw him move. (Lahiri, 18)

The question of identity is very crucial for immigrants. Lahiri explains that, "The question of identity is always a difficult one…those who grow up in two worlds simultaneously, as is the case for their children…I think that for immigrants, the challenges of exile, the loneliness, the constant sense of alienation, the knowledge of and longing for a lost world, more explicit and distressing then for their children." (2)

The duality of culture threatens Gogol's identity that is reflected in his personal relationship also. He experiences an emotional turbulence and is torn from inside by the mixed feeling of love and hatred for India. He is bewildered and unable to fully match up with Western culture. Neither his marriage with Moushmi nor his involvement with Ruth or even his passionate love affairs with young Maxine make him a happy man. In spite of his westernization, Gogol is not completely cut off from his roots and identity. Gogol rebels and changes his name as Nikhil, rejects the world of his parents but his refusal to recognize his past makes him a stranger to himself. However, the death of his father gives him a new beginning. He understands community feeling and place of family and an individual in the society. His relationship with Maxine comes in crisis when she does not understand the reason and emotion of his talk with his mother and sister every evening after the death of his father. She says, "You guys can't stay with your mother forever" (182) and further when she plans holiday to overcome the demise of father and emotional turbulence then Gogol replies "I don't want to get away" (182). Finally, he reclaims his own past and his true self emerges and integrates him with society. At the end of the novel, Gogol begins to read the story *The Overcoat* by Nikoloi Gogol that has been gifted to him by his father on his fourteenth birthday and that had been read by his father at the time of train crash.

Mira Nair has successfully captured immigrant psyche weaved in Lahiri's novel. She has worked on all the aspects of novel to transform it into film. Nair has not twisted prime plot of novel but employs cinematic liberty with an innovative exercise. She skips some details and introduces some brilliant nuggets of character and plot development to show the novel's narrative into two hours film. In the movie, she introduces Ashima as classical singer and repeats the train accident of Ashok again and again where Gogol gets his name in the film, while cuts so many pivotal dramatic sequences of the novel like Ashima misses her bag of shopping on the metro and for the first time she feels a kind of bondage to the city in strange way, when she gets back it from MBTA lost and found without missing a teaspoon. Lahiri writes: "Somehow, this small miracle causes Ashima to feel connected to Cambridge in a way she has not previously thought possible…" (42-43) but the very next day after hearing the demise of her father she deliberately leaves her shopping bag that shows her grief of being in the city that disconnects her to her family and root. Nair has done such mutation with incision and interpolation to fit the demands of time and audience.

Both the versions of *The Namesake* possess autobiographical touch. Lahiri being an Indian by ancestry, British by birth and American by immigration is well acquainted with the challenges or loneliness of the exile and longing for the lost world through her parents. Lahiri belongs to the second-generation immigrants, shares conspicuous similarities with the protagonist Gogol. In an interview by Houghton Mifflin, she admits it "I'm like Gogol in that my pet name inadvertently becomes my good name" further she accepts "…it bothered me growing up, the feeling that there was no single place, I was fully belonged". Similarly, Mira Nair identifies herself more with the protagonist Ashima. She reminisces in her interview by Aseem Chhabra that the "…image of Ashima in her sari, hauling her laundry cart in snow…reminds me when I came to the U.S." Nair shares her feeling that when in novel Ashima cries over the death of her close relatives and consoled by Ashok it feels a kind of solace to her. This novel brings her back to her creative root. Nikhat Kazmi reviews the film in the entertainment supplement of *The Times of India* 24 March 2007 that "*The Namesake* is Mira Nair's tribute to her janambhumi".

Film and fiction have different narrative codes. Film cannot present the action in the past in the same way as novel chiefly does. Lahiri's elusive third person narrative suits to the cultural conflicts dealt in the whole book. She has developed her own technique by shifting the mode of narration from past to present and vice versa. The third person narration is centred on Gogol/Nikhil's perspectives as Gogol's identity crisis is the focus of Lahiri. She pictures him as the victim of racism and on the margin of unwelcomed society. Occasionally, she gives the perspective of Ashima and Ashok and only one chapter is given to Moushmi's perspective, wife of Gogol who addresses him as Nikhil. Moushmi is confused regarding her past relations and marries to Gogol only because his change of name. Lahiri mentions: "…it was a thing that made him somehow new, not the person her mother had mentioned" (248). However, final two paragraphs of the novel are in future tense and narrator describes Gogol Ganguli in pronoun and his identity for future is opened:

> He will apologize…. He will walk downstairs with his mother, join the crowded party…anxious to return to his room, to be alone, to read the book he had once forsaken. (290)

Lahiri evokes meaning out of the symbolic descriptions. Sometimes she deliberately leaves to readers to unravel the meaning. She never directly depicts feeling and emotions of characters. Instead of grief in words Gogol's desolation at the loss of his father she describes through objects:

> He sees a pair of his father's and pair of flip-flops…four plates two mugs four glasses. In a drawer he finds one knife and two forks… in another cupboard are a box of tea bags, Peek Freans short bread biscuits, a five-pound bag of sugar that has not been poured into bowl, a tin of evaporated milk. (175)

However, filmic codes enable Nair to picturize such intricate narration and multicultural heterogeneity of the novel into a grand movie. In adaptation of the novel director in order to emulate the composition invents and arranges all the actors, scene and action, costume, music, etc. It is Nair's creativity that so many unforgettable scenes she has given in the movie dilating them from little descriptions in the novel. As Ashima unaware of Western style, washes Ashok's sweater in wash tub which shrinks and makes furious to Ashok. As a result she locks herself in the bathroom then he convinces her with love. Lahiri has thrown away some sentences without any thought of visualizing them. She appreciates Nair in her interview by Vibhuti Patel for the "scenes that came out of small details, throw away lines". The visit of Ganguly family to Taj Mahal and their conversation with each other is one of the touching scenes because it gives the emotion of nostalgia and inspires Gogol to be an architect.

In Lahiri's version, characters are not involved in deep conversation but Nair deploys human voice as a power to present human feelings and by making her characters to speak in Bengali, she makes them real. Lahiri accepts the power and appeal of visual art. She says that her characters "not real as actors made them on screen I have found my characters to speak in English…when I'm writing I hear the words in Bengali on my head…I loved (it)" (Patel's interview).

Ashima is the most evolved character which is shown in the film and novel both with her distortion and suffering. In the movie, Tabu matures from a young girl into a mother who raises her children with responsibility in a foreign land. Nair has planned casting perfectly; she has chosen Eastern and Western actors keeping in mind theme of the novel. Irrfan Khan, Tabu and Kal Penn have played major role. Besides them

Jacinda Barret as Maxine Ratliff and Zuleikha Robinson as Moushumi Mazumdar's roles are remarkable. In the novel and film both, the story revolves around Gogol and undoubtedly Kal Penn snatches attraction but through their quite, controlled and precisely nuanced performance Irrfan and Tabu convey the immigrant psyche that is purely incredible.

Music and soundtrack play very important role. It enriches the literary work by shedding new light on its "meaning, mood, and textuality" (Fulton 108). Movie begins and ends with songs. The fusion of classical and Western songs symbolizes struggle of family, moving between two worlds. Nair enchants the audience with vibrant Baul songs, Rabindra sangeet and Western rap music. With the help of costume, Nair narrates social and psychological position of the characters. In the film, Maxine clearly exhibits cultural difference when she comes to mourn the death of Gogol's father in black dress whereas grief-stricken family and whole Bengali community is in white. To present the regret of Gogol, Nair has skillfully invented and shown the saving of his head after his father's death.

Nair has edited space and time of the novel. The novel begins in 1967 and ends in 2000, while the film begins in 1977 and ends in 2004. The novel and film also take place in two different spaces. Lahiri narrates whole diasporic pain and pleasure on the spatial distance between India and America but Nair emphasizes the continuity between these two sites. She substitutes New York for Boston and establishes a visual continuity that binds together Calcutta with New York. Nair aims to shoot these two cities as if they are one. Through this technique, she highlights the in-between world of the migrants. Nair uses effectively camera technology to link together Ashok and Ashima's present existence in the United States with their memories of home in India. Each scene is amazingly true to life whether a scene on a Kolkata street, or in the United States, the ambience, the atmosphere, everything is perfectly picturized.

Both the creators, Lahiri and Nair facing dislocation from their motherland, caught between two worlds they convey their experiences of alienation with lucid perception. The literary works are natural expression of emotive feelings and consciousness of the author while film is technological dimension. Literary representation cannot take the place of visual imagination as both the mediums have different devices and strategies to appeal and enthrall the reader or audience. Nair has successfully turned Lahiri's elusive narration into motion picture and focused on poignant feelings of immigrant experiences with authentic locales, breathing character and cinematic codes. Nair seems remarkable in her presentation of Lahiri's text, she has not only reproduced and reduced book in camera culture to heighten the realism of the text but has exercised her creative faculty.

Works Cited

Fulton, Helen. "Film Narrative and Visual Cohesion." *Narrative and Media*. Ed. Helen Fulton. Cambridge: Cambridge University Press, 2005.

Lahiri, Jhumpa. An Interview with the Author. Houghton Mifflin. Web. 16 Jan. 2013.

—— *The Namesake.* London: Harper Collins, 2003.

—— "Its Mira Nair's Stamp on My Story". Web 16 Jan. 2013.

Nair, Mira. Interview by Aseem Chhabra. "Mira Nair: The Lesson of Our Parents". Web. 26 Jan. 2013.

Nikhat, Kazmi. "The Namesake Review". *Times of India*, 24 March 2007.

<http://timesofindia. indiatimes.com/entertainment/moviereviews/english/18026555.cms>

□

Patriarchy or Primitivism?: Violence in Vijay Tendulkar's *Silence! The Court is in Session*

Aindrilla Guin

Vijay Tendulkar, one of the most prominent dramatists in India, in his *Silence! The Court is in Session* (1971), the translation of the original Marathi version, *Santata! Court Chalu Ahe* makes a unique portraiture of a woman bubbling in life, slowly getting into a trap very cunningly crafted by her associates. The play sees a woman, Benare, who is a schoolmistress and one who claims herself to be dutiful and honest to her profession express herself boldly. This lady in the course of time is beguiled by a host of men and a woman. Benare, the same woman who speaks the most, insults and jeers at others, suddenly becomes the person who is interrogated, observed, contested till she is bared of her secrets. Benare bleeds, cries, laments in vain; a huge uproar is raised by those who have tracked her and they ultimately drag her to her fallen state. This paper keenly observes how the fall of Benare from her heightened status to her grovelling state is very much in the resemblance of a hunted animal, wild, powerful, yet defenceless before man's artful cunning. Popularly seen as a patriarchal text where the aspiring woman is made tame through a back breaking exercise in the form of a mock-interrogation, this paper deviates in its attempt from giving an insight into patriarchy's motives by exposing the primitive in man that hunts and kills, pursues and stabs for sport.

Tendulkar's play opens with Benare, making her first appearance with a village youth Samant in a room where the local bhajan group hold their programmes. As the two proceed in their conversation, we realise Benare is seducing the youth, though the seriousness of her motive remains in doubt. This apparently harmless and naive youth later on becomes an important witness in the mock trial by dint of which Benare is pinned down. In Tendulkar's play Benare the schoolmistress is also a member of the dramatic group performing the trial of President Johnson for producing atomic weapons. Benare comically enacts the roles of different characters and mocks the idiosyncrasies of the other members of the group.

The characters in this play mark a bipolar structure, in which Benare stands alone, but strong and powerful on the one hand, while on the other the rest of the members of the group who are far less efficient and ineffectively play their parts in their real life. The play sees a characteristic change of situation whereby the powerful suddenly becomes vulnerable and the less effective people come together to form a group who take Benare by surprise and close in upon her gradually. The noose gets tightened and Benare stands in a strait, where she is forced to confess her so-called sins. She is torn apart and her state becomes one that has lost its vigour and self-respect.

Now if we consider her case, Miss Benare is gang-raped in the hands of patriarchy. The entire train of men and Mrs Kashikar, all seize Benare for her illicit affair with a married man, Professor Damle, and for the illegitimate child in her womb. Benare is left to look out for a husband who would give her a legitimate status of a wife and her child the name of the father, which is the focus of patriarchy. Benare in spite of her justified claim of her supremacy over her inmates has to stand subordinate to the male members of her group. She had asked of favours of most of the men and had faced insults in the hands of many. Lastly, she is proved to have committed the blackest sin of corrupting motherhood. Finally the aspirant lady too is daubed in patriarchy for she asks not for a daughter, but consciously or unconsciously claims the child in her womb to be her "son". In no way can it be said that it is not a feminist text, a critique of patriarchy, this not only shows how the grim machinery of patriarchy sours the existence of the female but also how it terribly affects their thought line. Women like Mrs Kashikar and Benare are made to think like their male counterparts and lie crippled in the hands of society.

However this paper while keeping this interpretation intact, looks at *Silence! The Court is in Session* from a different perspective which finds this play as bearing the legacy of the age-old dramatic tradition of the Aryans. The Aryans, the warrior race took to hunting as their pastime and re-enacted their hunting process in their dramatic performances. Most actors either acted as hunters or different tame and wild animals.

Hunting was one of the most important forms of enunciating their daily activities, where the hunting of tame animals as goats, cows, monkeys, etc. by wild animals or the hunting of the wild animals by men, both became part of their play-act. As the *Indian News Reader* comments:

> The origin of the Indian theatre or rather folk theatre and dramatics can be traced to religious ritualism of the Vedic Aryans. This folk theatre of the misty past was mixed with dance, ritualism, plus a depiction of events from daily life. It was the last element which made it the origin of the classical theatre of later times. Many historians, notably D.D. Kosambi, Debiprasad Chattopadhyaya, Adya Rangacharaya, etc. have referred to the prevalence of ritualism amongst Aryan tribes in which some members of the tribe acted as if they were wild animals and some others were the hunters. ("Ancient Indian Theatre")

A similar note has been brought in by literaryblog—

> The dramatic performances of those times mainly included depiction of events of daily life accompanied by music. Some members of the tribe acted as if they were wild animals and some others were the hunters. Those who acted as animals like goats, buffaloes, reindeers and monkeys were chased by those playing the roles of hunters and a mock hunt was enacted. In such a crude and a simple way was drama performed during the age of the Vedic Aryans. Tendulkar's plays are not without the violence; more so violence is ingrained in his texts generating life force.

Literaryblogspot gives—Influenced by Artaud, Tendulkar relates the problem of anguish to the theme of violence in most of his plays. He does not consider the occurrence of human violence as something loathsome of digusting— "The spirit of aggression is something that human being is born with. Not that it is bad. Without violence man might have turned into a vegetable." This violence is perfectly enacted in minute detail in Silence!.

The play begins with Samant a village youth entering the hall that has two doors "One to enter by, and one to go to an adjoining room" (1). Immediately one is remembered of an emergency exit to escape. As the drama starts rolling Benare enters the hall sucking her fingertip. Samant tries to find out— "Did you catch your finger in the bolt? These old bolts are all the same. They just won't slide straight. And if the bolt stays out just a little bit, and you don't pull it clean to one side, then what happens?

Shut the door—and you've had it! Locked yourself in!" (1). The indication of being trapped and confiscated immediately comes to mind. Samant himself is carrying a toy parrot, and the presence of birds as sparrow and parrot is quite symbolic for they are often birds of prey.

As the play unfurls and the rest of the team members join Samant and Benare, the latter sounds quite confident, ebullient and happy to be herself. Her attitude towards Samant is overpowering and she tries to seduce Samant. But she is unaware of the trap lurking. The sense of being locked and locking oneself in becomes the leit-motif of the play. Benare claims, "I am feeling marvellous" (1) and such satisfying comments as "I felt even wonderful coming here with you" (1). Benare makes Samant intimidated by her presence; however she doesn't feel any fear in his company. Benare is lured by the apparently naive Samant; Samant acts as bait that entices and gradually draws Benare into the trap.

The play involves a host of people who individually or collectively drag Benare into a position where she unconsciously becomes the victim, the prey. She moves to the adjoining room and in that brief span the group device their advancing moves towards her. She is taken by chance and suddenly they take her capture. Benare comes out of the room, "singing, wiping her face on the towel. She looks very fresh" (23). Immediately Ponkshe stands before her, guarding her way, "Miss Leela Benare, you have been arrested on suspicion of a crime of an extremely grave nature, and brought as a prisoner before the bar of this court" (23). The immediate reaction as given in the stage direction is that of Benare stiffening—"She looks around her numbly". Ponkshe guards Benare, the trapped, with his gaze. While Benare is highly uncomfortable, the others made aware of her discomfiture take advantage of the situation. As the stage direction goes:

> Meanwhile, Kashikar comes and seats himself on the judge's chair on the dais. He signals to the people in the wings. Karnik and Rokde silently bring the wooden dock and arrange it around Benare. Sukhatme comes from the wings putting on his black lawyer's gown.... The others go to their places. Samant enters and stands in the doorway. (23)

This is an intricately crafted plan as not a single corner is left for Benare's escape. Though the people of the group arrive at different times and belong to the different strata of the society, all join hands to close Benare in. Benare is here the odd-one-out for she is the one who wants to live wild, free from the bonding of the society. Her nature too is wild and untamed and her passions are never tormented by the social taboos. The others on the contrary conform to the societal norms guided by patriarchy. If the people around her represent the Superego, the morality principle, Benare is Id, the seething cauldron of desire, the pleasure principle. Life brews animal instincts, power and energies in Benare. Benare's impulses are not guided by the codes of society, as she had fallen in love with her own maternal uncle proving that desire is not that which tutored and cultivated on the guidelines set down by the society, instead it is that which is naturally spurred and generated. She is never alarmed at the thought of incest propounded by society.

Whenever Benare speaks it is mostly in terms of her body. Her feelings, excitements, energies are mostly depicted through such expressions as "I'd give the last drop of my blood to teach them" (4); "It must mingle with your blood. It'll only stay once it's in your blood" (9). She cries aloud, laughs, boos one of her associates, and hides behind the door where her body touches Samant. Her playful discussions are about tongue and when she enters she is sucking her fingertip. She believes her "wishes" (5) are her own and "No one can kill those" (5). It is her life and her body she celebrates; she vaunts aloud, "I am not dead! Not dead!" (9). The attitude of her associates too exposes their expectation of savouring raw meat as Sukhatme confesses, "when there's a woman in the dock, the case does have a different complexion, that's true. That is my experience" (22).

In spite of her powers Benare's entrapment marks the vulnerability of animal existence in the hands of wily and crafty men. The mock trial scene is enacted with the purpose of making the real hunt—"The crime itself is imaginary.... Only the accused is real" (43). At the end of Act II, after Samant had produced his bit of fake-witness from the book by Suryakant Phatarphekar matching Benare's moral degradation. Benare literally tries to escape in vain.

> She goes towards the other door, and unbolts it. All are watching. The door does not open. She pulls at it. It will not open. She starts tugging at it hard. It is locked from outside. She bangs on it with vehemence. And louder. But it is locked. A peculiar joy begins to show on everyone's face but Samant's. (48)

Instead of characteristically showing his joy Samant shows his concern but the genuineness of the same remains in doubt. It was Samant's prediction that Benare would lock herself in if she did not pull the bolt to one side. His evidence is just another nail in Benare's coffin and as soon as Benare's locking up occurs, he claims: "There! It's happened! The bolt's slipped shut outside...you've had it! The door's locked from outside. Try as you will, it just won't open. And what's more, the offices are closed. So there won't be anyone outside just now" (48).

Samant had as if waited for this with bated breath and far from Benare's confinement having troubled him, he is confirmed in the pronouncement of Benare's lot.

With the opening of Act III, every garb of sophistication falls off the characters and they present themselves in their fierceness. Sukhatme has a "perverse excitement" (50) in his gleaming eyes and Mrs Kashikar drags Benare to the witness-box—"Benare's face reveals the terror of a trapped animal" (50). Sukhatme jerks his body like a wrestler in his new-found strength, as if on the verge of tightly securing his catch. He not only confronts her but scares her through his taking Benare unawares from the back. By this act Benare is thoroughly transformed into an animal and the hunters are led bare of their intentions. The sophistication of society has shorn off and the wrestler in man, duelling for his game stands without the mask. Just as a fierce repetition of the first Act, once again the characters conspire to keep her in the trap—"Benare leaves the witness-box and goes to the door. It is locked. Ponkshe blocks the way, so she turns aside. By then, Mrs Kashikar has caught hold of her, and leads her to the dock" (53).

As one proceeds in the play, the different stage directions describing Benare show Benare's categorical transformation from wildness to one grovelling in dust. The hunt is almost made and Benare is "hapless" (58), "stiffens" (58) and then "flinches" (59). Mrs Kashikar "looks daggers" (62) at Benare and in the course of action the latter, "struggles to her feet and tries to reach the door. Mrs Kashikar grasps her and forces her back to the dock" (67). As the play is about to end "Benare is motionless" (72), tries to make an attempt at standing up erect being motionless (72), and then, "[s]huts her eyes and mutters in mortal pain" (75). The locked door finally opens only after she had collapsed, "in paroxysms of torment with her head on the table, motionless" (76). Towards the closing of the play the characters gather around the motionless Benare and to console their conscience the characters claim:

> Sukhatme: "Just a game! What else? A game! Ponkshe: A mere game!" (77)

It is indeed very difficult to deny the possible pun in the word "game" where the sport of hunting and the hunted conflate in the different meanings of the same word. A sport for enjoyment that costs one to collapse and stiffen or rest motionless even after the fit is over is indeed too big for mere entertainment. Another word that makes a mark is the characters' (apart from Benare) leaving the stage in a "herd" (77). That they form one clan and Benare is not simply an oddity in the group becomes clear in her staying back where she had collapsed.

In the end Benare "feebly stirs a little. Then gives up the effort". We are not sure whether Benare is alive or dead. This is also in a way Tendulkar's "subconscious departure" (qtd. Bandyopadhyay xlviii) from realism through a symbolic enunciation of the hunt. Tendulkar himself speaks of an essential preying in his striking a similarity between Silence! And his other play *Gidhade* (*Vultures*)—"In *Gidhade* it is a pack of human vultures pitched against a defenceless female character, the wife of Ramakant. In *Shantata*, it is Miss Benare against a pack of middle-class vultures" (qtd. Bandyopadhyay xlix). The paper sees the text as open-ended leaving scope for both interpretations. The play is at once a gang rape of an aspirant woman by patriarchy, and the human hunt for the wild animal popularized as a part of both existence and show of power from time immemorial. Especially popularized by the Aryans and an important form and a subject of dramatic performance, Vijay Tendulkar in a way recoils upon a past tradition which is thoroughly Indian and at once an archetype.

Works Cited

"Ancient Indian Theatre". *Indian News Reader*. 14 Nov 2009. Web. 25 Nov 2015.

Bandyopadhyay, Samik. "Introduction". *Collected Plays in Translation: Vijay Tendulkar*. 2003; New Delhi: OUP, 2004. Print.

Tendulkar, Vijay. "Development of Indian English Drama". *Literaryindia.com*, 2011. Web. 29 Nov 2015.

——. *Silence! The Court is in Session*. 1978. Trans. Priya Adarkar. New Delhi: OUP, 2013. Print.

□

Jhumpa Lahiri's *Interpreter of Maladies*: A Reconfiguration of the Human Predicament

Reena Mitra

Scholars of literature are well aware of how fiction as a genre has, in most countries, contributed to the crystallization of the concept of a homogeneous state and community and how it has "traditionally been implicated in the construction and consolidation of the idea of a nation".[1] With this purpose of merger and fortification in view Indian writers of fiction in English, i.e. the novel and the short story, too, tend to project an unvaried and uniform picture of reality and incline towards blunting the edges of conflicting relations between individual non-conformists and communal entities in a pluralistic society. Jhumpa Lahiri, in her literary marvel, *Interpreter of Maladies*,[2] an award-winning anthology of short-stories published in the year 1999, specifically takes care to avoid essentializing her characters, be they Indians, Pakistanis, Indian-American or members of any other community that she can confidently write about. She seeks, as identified by a critic, "to study bewildered, withered, perplexed and grey shades of relationships and events present in the book".[3] And, the important issue in this reconfiguration of human relationships and predicaments is the need to arouse consciousness regarding the human situation and to change attitudes, to sensitize individuals to human pain and suffering, be it the pain of a migrant subjected to racial discrimination or the psychological or subconscious fears that plague one in the quotidian activities of life. Thus, Lahiri's texts symbolize the misery of lost voices and fading identities that need to be understood and reached out to for any kind of resuscitation. Any interpretation of Lahiri's stories has to be determined by the factors of human relatedness which govern the work and which, on balance, sway in the liminal space of being neither Indian nor of the diaspora. Lahiri offers images of deprivation in terms of a lost home and lost relationships. In the eponymous story entitled "Mrs. Sen's" the protagonist nostalgically tells her eleven-year-old-ward, Eliot, "everything is there" meaning India, but, boundaries—geographical, cultural and psychic—are receding; what preoccupies one's mind today is an existential distress caused by the essential human situation. Academic internationalism prevalent in the present times may, too, persuade one to brush aside local and culture-specific aspects and espouse all that stands for globalism, multilocality and multiculturalism. While talking about international themes, more particularly with reference to feminism, Malashri Lal states that "the 'home' is not so much a geographical place as it is an expression of identity strenuously won out of a series of conflictual confrontations...."[4]

And once this conflict is over, the crisis is over, and, there is a compromise that brings peace and a sense of equilibrium.

Cultural "other-ization" prevails when there is a shift in location from one's own social group to assume the status of a member of a minority community in an alien and multicultural society and we are, perforce, "unselved",[5] as Meena Alexander, herself a diasporic writer, puts it. Jhumpa Lahiri, a second-generation Asian American, does occasionally give evidence of a cultural schizophrenia but with the present global access to cultures and identities, and with blends of lifestyles emerging as a kind of acceptable option, she has graduated to an enigmatically composite stance in life whereby older venerable cultures acquire the facade and semblance of the newer ones that apparently overtake the earlier civilizational edification. This does not, however, imply that there will be any kind of attrition or obliteration of the essential cultural or civilizational differences perpetrated by passage of time and rooted in antiquity. Lahiri, despite being born and brought up in the United States, often gives expression to the "trailings" left behind in India like the "vanishings" of Wordsworth's "Ode to Immortality" which in her "doth breed perpetual benediction"[6] and aesthetic inspiration.

Diasporic writing often pushes one to ask a question raised by Derrida, "Where then are we? Where do we find ourselves? With whom can we identify in order to affirm our own identity...?"[7] And yet, despite the search for identity and the concomitant "trauma" and the "mourning" that are often referred to[8] as crystallizing the ordeal, diasporic writers like Jhumpa Lahiri have discovered avenues to surmount this consciousness of cultural deprivation and divert their aesthetic energies to so merge the homeland truths with the adopted and appropriated "aliveness" and lifestyle as to glide into a happy global domain in which

> diasporas and homelands may, paradoxically, come much closer to each other than ever before. Yet, this closeness will not necessarily camouflage their divergent interests or politics of representation.[9]

From the historical perspective, then, the long and eventful century of European political domination, and specifically, the British sway over a large number of countries in the world in the late nineteenth and early twentieth century left behind a civilizational repercussion, which people in the world are till date taking cognizance of for the continuities and transgressions are still of consequence in the reorganization of the decolonized societies. Postcolonialism, as and when it came, was not merely a chronological stage in the history of the world but a pronouncement of ideological deliverance from the Western modes and standards, especially for practitioners of the literary art for whom the slide from post-colonialism to the rather recent notions of globalization and multiculturalism has never been inconceivable. The acceptance and the realization has been very evident, almost palpable in their works. Postcolonialism in its onward journey has moved from the valorization of marginality to an endorsement of world denizenship.

The complex and enigmatic relationship between imperialism and postcolonialism has brought forth a situation in which any discourse on the latter is itself largely governed and steered by the very erstwhile sovereign culture it seeks to battle against and supplant. Academic queries cannot be sorted out without reference to the larger context of cultural, political, social and economic aspects of the times. This qualified civilizational interaction between India and the West with its characteristic nuances of existence has allocated to the former the grave charge of what Makarand Paranjape defines as "accepting our share of responsibility in the unfinished project of national and—if one can go that far—international reconstruction".[10]

Our enterprising diasporic writers like Salman Rushdie, Jhumpa Lahiri, Bharati Mukherjee, V.S. Naipaul, Rohinton Mistry, Vikram Seth, A.K. Ramanujan, Meena Alexander and Uma Parameswaran have taken up the gauntlet of confronting the complex cultural imperatives of adopting biculturalism as well as of reflecting a worldview that is "glocal" in terms of crystallizing problems encountered by mankind anywhere on earth. In the present context, the following statement of Paranjape is illustrative of the most workable resolution to the issues of diasporic writing:

> I consider biculturalism or multiculturalism to be somewhat like bilingualism or multilingualism—they involve the ability to be functional in or familiar with more than one culture, or, to use current economic parlance, cultural market.[11]

Choosing from the four probable styles of creative writing in Indian English literature enumerated by G.N. Devy one would be inclined to identify in Lahiri's works:

> ...the style in which internationalism and nationalism meet and collaborate, where the alien cultural features work together with the "marga" cultural features.[12]

The national or the "marga" features with their unmistakable indigenous appeal are seen, for example, in her food imagery that is typically Indian, and further, typically Bengali, Bengal being the region of her origin in India. Lahiri, like Raja Rao, a stalwart of Indian English fiction, combines in her style, a strain of existentialism characteristic of international writing in general with a touch of the emotional and the sentimental, which though largely subdued, is indisputably there.

Style apart, Jhumpa Lahiri's *Interpreter of Maladies* is rich in thematic content and the protagonists of her short stories are individuals one can identify and empathize with. Despite being a "hybrid-realization" of the characteristic migrant experience and of "a sort of half-way feeling", the stories are conspicuously about the complex texture and inner recesses of human nature and the quintessence of individual sentience. Though it is primarily Lahiri's exhaustive understanding of the migrant situation that is rendered in her work, the "miscommunication" within the self and its reverberations in human relationships could be applicable inclusively to immigrants anywhere in the world. In her observant exposition of the singular human predicament and proclivities, she has chosen a genre—the short story—which is relatively incapacious and inextensible in scope, yet, in spite of her limited canvas she has effectively initiated the uninitiated into an exploration of the identity of the self and the existential dilemma stalking man in every option he exercises.

Lahiri, generally believed to be a spokesperson of the Indian diasporic Wordsmiths writing in English, and often hailed as a feminist, is primarily, by her own confession, an author who deals in human "maladies" pervading "Bengal, Boston and Beyond", with "Beyond" signifying the essential human situation prevailing anywhere and everywhere that human life exists. The imaginative reconstruction of such situations marked by vividness and verisimilitude is what makes her stories worth reading. Shashi Deshpande, however, expresses a grave doubt about the reliability of stories relating to India written by writers settled abroad:

> ... What troubles me even more is what I call 'writing from memory'.... Does the memory get crystallized or fossilized? And how does one continue to write about a life and society without being an intrinsic part of its daily living, its dynamism.[13]

Lahiri, however, seems to have been in frequent touch with her relatives in Kolkata in India and had resolutely visited her grandmother here almost every year, keeping as close as possible to the "living" experience of life in Bengal.

Jhumpa Lahiri is a writer with a firm, unfaltering gaze that penetrates deep into the world and its inhabitants. She sincerely respects the myriad aspects of this world, never losing consciousness of its vastness and variety. Her plots are elegantly constructed and revolve around protagonists who are mostly immigrants trying to relocate themselves in a foreign land and their minds are engagingly depicted as caught between the past and the present, the traditional and the modern and the native and the alien.

The subtle expose of the underlying meaning of her stories through uncomplicated and simple plots and characters lends a rare sophistication to Lahiri's narrative art and what attracts us most in these tales is "The extraordinariness of the experience evoked by the ordinariness of expression."[14] The stories either reveal the inner recesses and principal features of the protagonist's character or chart the evolution of the central character in each story. Some of these stories often present a sudden transformation in the basic tendencies of an individual. The formula suggested for resolving problems in life is a mutually beneficial blending of the best in the East and the West, the worst in both having been discarded. Lahiri's is an art in which the mode of communication is that of silences rather than of speech. She subjects her characters to the contemporary situation and explores the depths of their hearts. In the course of this scrutiny and soul-searching, she initiates the reader into an existentialistic labyrinth where reflections of one's own true nature may be identified.

Lahiri's stories are mostly depictions of human misery and desperation. The first story in the anthology, *Interpreter of Maladies*, is "A Temporary Matter" in which a young Indian American couple strives to contend with a failed marriage and the loss of a child at birth six months ago. There is a kind of estrangement that has set in between the two who now labour to avoid each other, Shoba preoccupying herself with work outside the house and Shukumar confining himself to one room and deliberately delaying the completion of his dissertation. A five-day power-cut for a specific period of time each day is announced by the authorities and the husband and wife are thrown in together in the house at the time of the outages. This forced companionship between the two encourages in them a degree of intimacy not indulged in since the death of their child. Communication had broken down and the silence that prevailed had begun to gnaw at them. As the darkness that prevails enables them to muster courage to face each other they divulge their painful secrets—Shukumar tells Shoba about the sex of the child they had lost though the latter had forbidden him to do so; Shoba on, the other hand, tells her husband of her firm decision to dissolve the marriage. Environment and darkness provide momentum to the plot; and food, an important signifier of Indian culture, is joyfully indulged in by both in happier times. The typical Indian "chutneys" referred to are part of an Indian American couple's meal in the United States—the blend from Bengal in India transcends boundaries to be part of an Indian American meal!! Jhumpa Lahiri's own life-experiences and predicaments provide the themes for this anthology of short-stories, food and cultural hybridity being some of them. Also, the story illustrates the fact that to the Indian psyche a child cements the bond of marriage, which is not merely a collaborative sexual alliance between two spouses but and indefinable relationship.

"When Mr. Pirzada Came to Dine", the second tale of the collection, is not as poignantly poised as the first is. The protagonist in this story is not from India but from Bangladesh, pursuing research in America. He was a frequent visitor to an Indian family in Boston. His primary concern at that time was the safety of his wife and seven daughters back home during the 1971 war for Independence in Bangladesh. The story is narrated from the perspective of Lilia, an impressionable young girl, who is only vaguely conscious of her cultural origin. While missing his daughters Mr. Pirzada rivets his love and affection on Lilia, who is perplexed at what she calls the "theatricality of his attentions" (29). Though still too young to understand the problems of life, Lilia is observant enough to see the human kind unite in a time of crisis.

> Most of all I remember the three of them operating during that time as if they were a single person sharing a single man, a single body, a single silence and a single fear. (41)

The predicament Mr. Pirzada finds himself in is unstintingly shared by Lilia's parents, who are able to identify and empathize with him in his extreme anxiety regarding the security of his family at home. It does not matter that Mr. Pirzada is from another country—his sentiments are unreservedly shared by this Indian family in Boston.

The typical Indian food offered to Mr. Pirzada even in Boston adds a dimension of the "glocal". Food habits are again, indicative of "the cultural roots of people. Lilia watches her mother bring forth the succession of dishes: lentils with fried onions, green beans with coconut, fish cooked with raisins in a yoghurt sauce" (30).

The title story, "Interpreter of Maladies" is about an expatriate Indian family from Boston visiting India to tour Odisha. The interpreter, Mr. Kapasi, is the tourist guide as well as the car driver. Mrs. Das praises Mr. Kapasi's work as an interpreter, though the latter's wife never appreciates his competence. This tacit understanding between Mrs. Das and Mr. Kapasi both of whom bear the cross of an indeterminately unhappy marriage, brings the two close and in a burst of intimacy the former tells the latter that one of her sons, Bobby, is not Mr. Das' son but of a Punjabi friend of his who had come to stay with them when Mrs. Das had given in to the lure of a purely sexual relationship. She confides in him in the hope that he would suggest some way of escaping from the sense of guilt she has been co-existing with for years for she, being an Indian, has been unable to shed her Indian consciousness which endorsed that women should be true to their husbands. It is this dichotomy one needs to overcome in trying to espouse a global approach though it is difficult to get out of one's native skin.

"A Read Durwan" is the story of an old watch woman popularly addressed as Boori Ma, who is eventually thrown out of the building she guards despite her sincerity because a theft has taken place there and she is suspected of having committed it. The only irksome trait of Boori Ma's character is that she is very loquacious and invariably boasts of her privileged past though none has ever corroborated this. The story is set in Bengal and has reminiscences of Tagore's poem, "Puratan Bhrutuyu" (the old servant), though Boori Ma, unlike the old servant, shows no signs of being dim-witted. This story portrays merely an incident and a character recreating the aura of Bengal.

The next story in the anthology, "Sexy", is about an extra-marital relationship that repulses Laxmi, an Indian-American: Miranda gets involved with Dev, a married man, in London. Indians settled abroad cannot accept this relationship because of the inveterate conservative mindset they possess. The climax is reached when Rohin, son of Laxmi's cousin, asks Miranda to wear a particular dress and then tells her "you are sexy". On being asked the meaning of the word "sexy" Rohin vaguely answers, "It means loving someone you don't know". (107). He further says, "That's what my father did.... He sat next to someone he didn't know, someone sexy, and now he loves her instead of my mother" (108). This brought an end to Miranda's affair with the married Dev for she realized the folly and immorality in human surrender to sexual urges. Human emotions are the same the world over and no woman likes to be targeted for reasons of sexuality alone. One often observes a touch of irony in Lahiri's stories though no explicit comments are ever made.

In "Mrs. Sen's", the crux of the matter for the protagonist seems to lie in the three-word communication, "Everything is there", the "there" here being a reference to India, a panacea to which she could revert whenever things became difficult for her. Mrs. Sen finds it very difficult to assimilate the lifestyle of the country of her adoption. Her job-requirement of baby-sitting and child-minding is learning how to drive and it is this that causes her tremendous distress as she just cannot take to the wheel. Married to a teacher of Mathematics in America, she does make perfunctory half-hearted efforts to conform to her acquired surrounding but never stops complaining about her discomfiture there and keeps telling her ward, Eliot, that for her "home" was India from memories of which her soul sought incessant nourishment. Her traditional Indian way of dressing up and of cooking especially fish, never let her forget her roots and she continues to experience a sense of nostalgia for the country of her birth. Yet, Eliot never fails to respond to the warmth and affection offered by her to him, especially when his own mother was uninvolved in any show of affection for him.

"The Blessed House" is the house at Connecticut of the newly-wed couple, Sanjeeb and Twinkle, the latter bring in the process of completing her master's at Stanford and trying to conclude her thesis on an Irish poet of dubious repute. Sanjeeb's parents were in India and Twinkle's had settled in California, though her name was indicative of her Indian connection for Douglas and Nora had never heard of it in America. The new house was a blessed one for Twinkle because she had found statues of Christ and Mother Mary in it and the switch plates in the bedrooms had scenes from the Bible on them. For Twinkle this focus on and display of these items in the house was an attention—grabbing exercise to impress the Americans; Sanjeeb as an executive in a firm, did not really care for these curios in the house but tolerated them because of Twinkle. That Sanjeeb and Twinkle as partners in a marriage are, in temperament, diametrically opposed is evident from their tastes and preferences. The religious icons Twinkle is obsessed with Sanjeeb finds irksome.

"The Blessed House" is one more instance of Lahiri's exploration of the theme of love and marriage where Sanjeeb's acquiescence in everything Twinkle does is only to buy peace and happiness in a marital alliance.

"The Treatment of Bibi Haldar", a story based in Bengal, is a poignant tale recounting the plight of Bibi Haldar who suffered from an indeterminate kind of ailment which no one was able to diagnose. Bibi Haldar was living with her relation in a flat in Calcutta and was given a claustrophobic, ill-equipped storeroom as accommodation. She was entrusted with the work of maintaining the inventory of the items in the cosmetics shop run by her cousin, Haldar. In return for her work, she was given food, shelter and clothing. Her obsession in life was to acquire a husband and go through the drills of a marriage ceremony. Mrs. Haldar, the owner's wife, was in the family way and considered Bibi Haldar as an evil omen who might bring harm to her child. A daughter born to Mrs. Haldar suffered illness for five days; it is then that the Haldar couple decided to wind up their work and leave the place. Bibi was left behind with a meager sum of three hundred rupees to survive on. After the departure of the Haldars, the story took a turn—mysteriously enough Bibi Haldar was found to be pregnant but a search for the man responsible for her conception was of no avail. She delivered a male child and "she was to the best of her knowledge, cured" (172).

The element of mystery in the story and the open-ended conclusion in it lends a peculiar interest to the narration. Though Bibi's ailment is never diagnosed, the cure that is eventually suggested is "relations". That the child "cures" Bibi at the end is an engrossing fact that leaves one thinking. Though earlier seen as not worthy of marriage, yet with the birth of the child and with being on her own, Bibi assumes all responsibilities expected to be discharged by a mother. The story speaks volumes for the power of women if and when fortified with opportunity and trust. The mystery man responsible for Bibi's being pregnant remains a secret till the end.

"The Third and Final Continent", the final story in *Interpreter of Maladies,* speaks affirmatively and happily of the migrant status of people in America. The narrator nostalgically recalls his school days in London spent with other expatriate Bengalis as room-mates. After his wedding he looks forward to his future in the United States. The story is one of slow and gradual acclimatization to an unfamiliar society where the protagonist goes all out to be part of the country of adoption. He sees in his hundred and three year-old-landlady, Mrs. Croft, an image of his mother back home and remembers the latter's last days with painful precision. The experience of relocating in a foreign place has been endowed by Lahiri with a kind of cumulative internalization that emerges from the protagonist's initial agonies and ecstasies lent focus by graphic descriptions. What endeared Mrs. Croft to the young Bengali commerce graduate was the feeling of kinship generated by his observation of her conservative views. She did not believe in a permissive society and disapproved of her daughter talking to the bachelor tenant for a long time. The protagonist soon moves house as his wife, Mala, joins him from India; thirty years down the line, he is still in America but rooted in his own country as well, and not without nostalgic memories of London—a man born of three continents!!

Interpreter of Maladies is a kaleidoscope of varied hues of human relationships and the human predicament. Lahiri's eye penetrates deep into the human psyche and its situations to make sense of the opportunities and dilemmas faced in an unknown world. Her stories deal with a motley collection of protagonists who hail from different countries but feel alike as human beings transcending the barriers and boundaries of geography, history and culture and conquering the fear of alienation and isolation. As postcolonial literatures highlight the diversities of ethnicity, religion, politics and lifestyle, Jhumpa Lahiri's book, placed in an international context, aims at a new cultural synthesis that happily accepts plurality as a path to global sympathy and empathy among peoples of different nations and countries.

Works Cited

Alexander, Meena. "Is there an Asian American Aesthetics?" *SAMAR* (South Asian Magazine for Action and Reflection). Winter, 1992: 26-27.

Derrida, Jacques. *Monolingualism of the Other or The Prosthesis of Origin.* Trans. Patrick Mensah. Stanford: Stanford University Press, 1998: 55.

Deshpande, Shashi. "Where do We Belong?". *Writing from the Margin.* New Delhi: Penguin, 2003: 49.

Devy, G.N. "Multiculturalism". *In Another Tongue.* Madras: Macmillan, 1995: 17 (rpt.).

Kishore, Paridhi. "Tracing Eccentricity in Jhumpa Lahiri's *Interpreter of Maladies*: Into Sere and Yellow Leaf". *Contemporary Indian Women Writers: Concepts and Contexts.* Eds. Nazneen Khan and S.G. Puri. New Delhi: Authorpress, 2014: 196.

Lahiri, Jhumpa. *Interpreter of Maladies.* New Delhi: Harper Collins, 1999.

Lal, Malashri. "Multilocality: International Themes in Women's Short Stories in English". *Signifying the Self.* Eds., Malashri Lal, Panja and Satpathy. New Delhi: Macmillan India Ltd., 2004: 152.

Mishra, Vijay. "Diasporas and the Art of Impossible Mourning". *In Diaspora.* Ed., Makarand Paranjape. New Delhi: Indialog Publications Pvt. Ltd., 2001. 33-35.

Mukherjee, Meenakshi. "The Anxiety of Indianness". *The Perishable Empire.* New Delhi: Oxford University Press; 2000; rpt. 2004: 173.

Paranjape, Makarand. "Introduction". *In Diaspora.* Ed., Makarand Paranjape. New Delhi: Indialog 2001: 12.

——. "Coping with Post-colonialism." *Interrogating Post-colonialism: Theory, Text and Context.* Eds. Harish Trivedi and Meenakshi Mukherjee. Shimla: Indian Institute of Advanced Study, 1996: 37, 47

Ramanarayan, Gowri. "Elegant Outsider". *The Hindu,* Literary Review. April 16, 2000: IX.

Wordsworth, William. "Intimations of Immortality from Recollections of Early Childhood". *The English Parnassus.* Eds. Dixon and Grierson. London: Oxford University Press, 1909; rpt. 1952: 320, ll. 33-34.

□

Evam Indrajit—And [One More] Indrajit: Role of Hindi Translations and Productions in Popularising Badal Sircar throughout India

Tapu Biswas

The eminent talented Hindi writer Dr. Pratibha Agarwal, who translated *Evam Indrajit* into Hindi, wrote in one of her major articles: "My Hindi version of *Evam Indrajit* was staged several times, thus making Badal Sircar popular throughout the country, and bringing due credit to me too." Rightly so. Those Indian litterateurs who did not know Bengali but aspired to translate *Evam Indrajit* into languages of their regions found Pratibha Agarwal's Hindi translation as a handy source. The present research paper discusses in detail what role the Hindi translations and productions of this work played in quickening the pace of popularity of its author, Badal Sircar, in the country.

Badal Sircar was a successful and influential town planner who felt inspired to turn to playwriting. However, in the early stages he continued to come up with some sorts of hilarious comic plays, a sort of a combination of fantasy and near-fact, perhaps written in the best tradition of comedies of Jyotindranath Tagore, Amritalal Bosu and other nineteenth-century Bengali playwrights. To the surprise of the theatre lovers, the tables turned when, surprisingly enough, in 1965, the reputable Bengali theatre journal *Bohurupee* carried a new play by Badal Sircar called *Evam Indrajit*.[1] It soon became a well-known name in theatre circle in India and was translated into Hindi and few other Indian languages and staged in many part of Indian country.

> The essential of the style—the same characters acting in several roles, the back and forth movement from the present—have been adopted

> since then in other plays. But in 1965, for the Bengali audience, *Ebong Indrajit* was a sort of invitation to an adventure in style.
>
> More important of course was the philosophical import. Here perhaps, for the first time in a Bengali play, was an attempt to present the existentialist question about the purpose of life. Artists had eternally addressed themselves to the question and had their own reasonable answer. Badal Sircar also provided an old answer, perhaps only by rephrasing it. Like Camus's *Sisyphus,* the alienated intellectual, the Indrajits, who know the futility of living, are doomed to continue living. The journey is more important than the destination.... Apart from the stylistic innovations of bold movements from one role into another, and of the daring liberties with time and space, *Ebong Indrajit* revealed another side of the playwright—his poetry. Some of the most beautiful lines have been given by the writer in the play, who breaks out into poetry to support his commentary on the action of the play, as a sort of aside to the audience.[2]

Thus, *Evam Indrajit* became a modern classic in every sense of the word and it was [and is] one play which caught a dilemma of Indrajit of our generation.[3] The well-known Hindi theatre director and actor Satyadev Dubey rightly observed: ...Badal Babu's entry into Indian theatre was beautifully timed. Perhaps he made the final breakthrough when a considerable amount of modernity had already been assured in and a new director who responded so happily to him had already achieved an identity.[4]

To further understand the impact of this play (viz. *Evam Indrajit*), it will be most relevant to refer here to what Girish Karnad (who translated this play into literary English) said about it in the Introduction to his translation:

> Writing about Badal Sircar's *Evam Indrajit* (literally, 'And Indrajit') is like going on a sentimental journey; a nostalgic foray into the recent past of the Indian theatre; an encounter with the bitter-sweet memories of a struggling sensibility trying to strike roots in a barren land; because, after all, it is only in relation to Indian theatre history that *Evam Indrajit* really makes its presence felt; otherwise it is just a very good, sensitively written play, like many others written in the last decade in India....

> The year 1962 is important to India for many reasons. 1962 was a year of great political turmoil. But it was also the year when Dharamvir Bharati's Hindi play *Andha Yug* was performed by Theatre Unit (Bombay). *Andha Yug* was a small beginning but the seeds of creative pride had been sown and a determined effort at looking at one's surroundings was to become an imperative which went beyond the platitudinous slogan of seeking one's roots. The imperative found its first fully conscious expression the same year in Calcutta, where a lean and balding Bengali architect was fulfilling his assignment as an urban designer and also writing a play, later to be recognized as a milestone in the history of modern Indian drama. The play was *Evam Indrajit*, written in Bengali by Badal Sircar....[5]

With the performance of Sircar's *Evam Indrajit* in Bengali in Calcutta in September 1965, theatre practitioners all over India became aware of a major talent and a major play. The play provided for them the shock of recognition. It was about the Indian reality as they knew it; it was a theatrically effective and crystallized projection of all the prevalent attitudes, vague feelings and undefined frustrations gnawing at the hearts of the educated urban middle class.

The first Hindi translation of this play was done in 1967 by Ram Gopal Bajaj, noted scholar, theatre director, academician and a Hindi film actor. He had also been a faculty member and a director of the National School of Drama, New Delhi from 1995 to 2001. For his contribution to theatre he was awarded the Sangeet Natak Akademi Award in 1996 and Padma Shri in 2003. The distinguished Hindi poet and translator Bharat Bhushan Agarwal (1919-75), also known for his work with the All India Radio and Sahitya Akademi, helped him to translate the poetic part of the texts. This Hindi version by Ram Gopal Bajaj formed the basis for the first ever Hindi production of the play by noted theatre director, actor and playwright Mohan Maharishi (a recipient of Sangeet Natak Akademi award). This maiden production of *Evam Indrajit,* in Hindi (just only about a fortnight after the original Bengali version), at Manzar Theatre, Pragati Maidan, New Delhi, under the aegis of the Delhi theatre group 'Yatrik', received notice at the national level but caught up in controversy because the producer-director changed the ending. In this production, different roles were performed by such seasoned and talented actors as Om Shivpuri, Sudha Shivpuri, B.M. Badola, Ram Gopal Bajaj, Dinesh Thakur, B.P. Sinha and Anjala Maharishi. Set design was by Mohan Maharishi, costumes by Anjala Maharishi, lights by V. Ramamoorthy. [It may be noted here that the theatre group 'Yatrik' had been founded by such scholars and theatre enthusiasts as Joy Michael, Rati Bartholomew, Roshan Seth, Sushma Seth, Marcus Murch, with active participation also of Bhaskar Ghose (of the Indian Administrative Service,—who later served as the Director General of Doordarshan, the Indian public television network) and some great amateur actors of the time like Kusum Haidar. It remained a forceful group which involved almost every noteworthy name in the Indian theatre of the time—acting, directing or even working backstage in its productions.] Reminiscing on the outrageous controversies that emerged, Mohan Mahirishi wrote:

> It was in the early 60's that some very exciting playwrights suddenly and simultaneously erupted on the national scene. [One of these was Badal Sircar]... Badal Babu's *Evam* had a breath of fresh air. Neatly written and unpublished Bengali text fell into our hands. Dr. Bharat Bhushan Agarwal and Ram Gopal Bajaj translated *Evam* directly from Bengali and I directed it for Joy Michael's Yatrik. Cast was stupendous. Om and Sudha Shivpuri, V.M. Badola, Ram Gopal Bajaj and Dinesh Thakur, formed the team which worked tirelessly under me for three months. The production immediately became controversial as I had outraged the theatre fraternity and well heeled critics by deleting all the poetry of Badal Babu and completely re-writing the third act. Sparse text, strong action and brutally stark visuals shocked the audience. But what shocked me was the outrageous response from theatre people. Back-bitten and foul-mouthed, I reveled in the controversies of the sixties.[6]

The Drama critic of the prestigious theatre journal *Enact* unequivocally voiced his appreciation of this first Hindi version of the play:

> The Hindi translation is remarkably well-done: the dialogue, rich in its use of phrases and idioms from spoken, often colloquial, speech, is adequately expressive. Frequently, certain familiar words through stylized repetitions emerge as effective symbolic scenes. But it is noteworthy that the symbols, verbal or visual, do not clog the fluidity of rendering; on the contrary, they add a force to the whole movement which one can without much effort call balletic.[7]

The same reviewer also gave the readers thought-provoking observations on the play:

> The Bengali drama, as Bengali life and literature in general, has admirably assimilated Western influences. Hindi drama, on the other hand, is still rather naïve, even Peter Panish for it almost refuses to grow. It toys with imitations and translations, but when it comes to doing something of its own it only dribbles, mumbles and stumbles. Even Mr Alkazi's best productions to date are mere translations, and it is much the failure of the National School of Drama as the failure of the Hindi language and literature that not a single playwright of any worth has yet come up.
>
> It is in this context…that Yatrik's *Indrajit* was a very bold venture, the kind of which has never been attempted on the Hindi stage. To Hindi speaking people, familiar with and therefore and always expecting sentimental screeching or hopelessly facetious and farcical drama, *Evam Indrajit* must naturally have appeared an enigma. Unable to co-operate with the play-in-performance which would have revealed to them the form and meaning of the seemingly disjointed snippets of dialogues and succession of scenes, they might being even have felt the affront of having ignored or cheated. This explains why Yatrik's play, despite its being an all-round perfect production drew a very thin audience, and eighty-five percent of it consisting of non-Hindi speaking people.
>
> *Evam Indrajit* tells the sad tale of a playwright who struggles painfully to write a play but cannot. He cannot because, as a conscientious and honest artist, he finds that 'life', the material of any art, is too chaotic and fragmentary to cohere into a dramatic mould and too mechanical to have any meaning. His agony is the agony of the artist who is deeply aware of the sterility and horror that is life today and yet gropes for a form and a meaning. Badal Sircar, the Bengali writer of the original play, offers no hope: the playwright character of *Evam Indrajit* ultimately meets with only despair, the keynote of which is struck in the beginning. But between the beginning and the end the play's action is the playwright's exploration of Indrajit who strikes him as a distinctly individual character among a group of indistinct, lifeless, blunt people going round and round the dull routine of life as unfeeling thick-skinned creatures. From the moment the playwright encounters Indrajit, Amal,

Bimal and Kamal, he begins to write his play trying to explore for some meaning in Indrajit's life as it grows through his college days, his youthful love of a girl and his rebellion against the whole set of social and moral conventions. But the social grinders begins to curse him gradually. Amal, Bimal and Kamal readily become the cogs in the wheel and they "flourish" materially. Indrajit, actually human, preservers to know the meaning of his own and their actions, the meaning of academic learning, of the day-by-day life, of love and marriage, of profession and practice and of money and happiness, and resists becoming a cog—as long as he can. The playwright grows hopeful of having at last found a hero for his drama; but soon his hope comes to nought. For Indrajit too ultimately wearies of resisting any longer. He is also desiccated of the urge to live a meaningful life; and gradually accepts becoming one like Amal, Bimal and Kamal (Nirmal he calls himself, to rhyme with the others). It is at this stage that the playwright kills Indrajit (though it is not in the script); but he in fact destroys once again his another attempt to write a play. The play thus progresses on two levels: the level of reality and of imagination, and both the levels come frequently close to one another, interpenetrate, tear apart and merge again. On the one hand the story of Indrajit, Amal, Bimal and Kamal is as real as that of the playwright with whom the play opens; on the other, the whole story of these characters is merely a projection of the playwright's creative mind preoccupied with yet another attempt to piece together the splinters of these lives to make a kind of architectural whole. Mr. Mohan Maharishi's production succeeded immensely in manipulating these two levels of the play. At the end, the two levels fuse indistinguishably: the murder of Indrajit is in fact an act of suicide committed by the playwright: it is the death-cry of the artist in him.

Evam Indrajit, however, suffers indubitably when compared to Pirandello's *Six Characters in Search of an Author*. For although in Badal Sircar's play it is the author, who is in search of characters, the thematic technique is basically the same: the confusion of the two levels of reality and illusion. But it suffers not because of a too highly developed and complex technical method employed to communicate themes which in the last resort are basically social, the evils primarily of urban industrialized society, shackled by inhuman convention, and they may well call for Ibsen's or Chekhov's dramatic methods. There are very few moments in the play when it seems to touch upon the fundamental, and therefore universal, phenomenon of the slow but steady dehumanization of a man's soul. But this is by no means a limitation of the play: even as it is, it is at moments not far from approximating to the phenomenon.[8]

Yatrik's Production of *Evam Indrajit*

This translation by Ram Gopal Bajaj, though not barred from being staged at Delhi under the direction of Mohan Mahirishi,[9] could not be made available in published form, because the author of the play, viz. Badal Sircar, had already signed a contract, giving permission for publication of Hindi translation to another scholar-translator, Pratibha Agarwal. However, in the year 2008, on the occasion of a 'Translation

Seminar' organised by Natya Shodh Sansthan at Kolkata, Ram Gopal Bajaj goodheartedly presented a Xerox copy of his translation (made in 1967) for being preserved in the archives of the Sansthan for use of visiting researchers.

Since the writer of the play had already given copyright permission to Pratibha Agarwal for a Hindi rendering of the play, she published her translation in 1969 through the then well-known publisher of Hindi books, Rajkamal Prakashan.

In her Translator's note Pratibha Agarwal observed:

> ...the reason for this popularity of *Evam Indrajit* is the specific specialized character both of his narration and style. This play has given a very realistic description of the ambition of youth of today (and probably of every age) and their subsequent disillusionment and disappointment. Though we know quite well that we have nothing to lean upon for purposes of living—no belief, no faith, no love —yet we must live. Knowing fully well that on the completion of our journey we will not have the celestial world before us, we must continue working because the road is there before us.[10]

In a review of this translation published in *Natrang* [Part IV, No. 14, April-June, 1970: 45-48] the reviewer noted that "this translation is quite close to the original. While Pratibha Agarwal immortalized this major play of Badal Sircar through her Hindi version, Satyadev Dubey and Shyamanand Jalan, through their productions of this play, injected a new idiom in the Hindi theatre production of the time."

It is significant that Pratibha Agarwal's Hindi translation formed a very solid foundation not only for various production of this play in Hindi in various areas of India but also for the renderings of the play in some other languages of the country. As we will see here later, Pratibha Agarwal remained so obsessed with the plays of Badal Sircar that she made it a life long ambition to render several of his other plays into Hindi. Apart from *Prabaser Hiji-biji* (written in diary style prose and verse) she translated into Hindi ten of his plays—a massive creditable achievement. As she herself later noted elsewhere,[11] her Hindi version was staged several times, thus making Badal Sircar popular throughout the country, and thus bringing due credit to her too. It may be noted here that Pratibha Agarwal, being in her own right a talented Hindi writer, injected into her translations a literary style of her own. Her translations are not couched in the routine prosaicrun-of-the-mill language but are in themselves a sort of literary works. Shyamanand Jalan observed:

> ...Dr. Pratibha Agarwal's translation was heavily Sanskriticized. Even I could not follow many of the poetic portions. So I had to make them intelligible to the audience which did not consist entirely of intellectuals, without sacrificing the basic import of the play. When you say, '*Klant, Klant, main bahut Klant hoon*', meaning I am very tired, you show 'klant' itself as a character speaking these words....[12]

Coincidentally, interestingly enough, Anamika Kala Sangam and Adakar in Calcutta, and groups like Dishantar and Abhiyan which enriched Delhi's stage, were also formed in the same year (viz. the year in which 'Yatrik' was established).

The first known stage production of Pratibha Agarwal's Hindi version of *Evam Indrajit* was in 1968 by 'Anamika', a theatre group co-founded [jointly with Pratibha Agarwal] by Shyamanand Jalan who is credited for the renaissance period of modern Indian theatre and specially the blossoming of Hindi theatre in Kolkata from the 1960s to 1980s. He was the first to perform modernist Mohan Rakesh's *Ashadh Ka Ek Din* [*One day in Ashadh*] in 1960 and subsequently laid down an excellent massive bridge between the Hindi and the Bengali theatre by mounting Hindi productions of Badal Sircar's *Evam Indrajit* (1968) and *Pagla Ghoda* (1971). Anamika's production of *Evam Indrajit* brought well-deserved fame to both Shyamanand Jalan and Anamika. It was adjudged as a production nearest to the idea of the playwright. The sets were designed by Khaled Chowdhury. Anamika toured various parts of the country with the play. In 1972, a special performance of *Evam Indrajit* was arranged with Satyadev Dubey, the noted director, actor, in the role of Indrajit and Jalan acting as Lekhak. The brilliant performance by both was remembered for years to come. The play was produced again in Delhi in 1973 when Shyamanand Jalan received the Sangeet Natak Akademi award for 1972. It was also telecast on the occasion.

The various roles in this performance were played by Satyadev Dubey/ Kalyan Chatterji (Indrajit), Shyamanand Jalan (Lekhak), Vimal Lath (Amal), Amar Gupta (Bimal), Arvindan (Kamal), Chetna Tiwari (Manasi).

In its Issue no. 25-26 (January-February 1969), the *Enact* Drama reviewer noted:

> Shyamanand's production of Badal Sircir's *Evam Indrajit* was an experience. Of the four different productions that I have seen—two Bengali and two Hindi, Anamika's production is the most imaginative; at the same time it is also the one truest to the script. In Nandikar's production, the writer (as played by Govind Ganguly) became more of a sissy; in Yatrik's production, as played by Om Sivpuri, he became an frustrated angry old man, diffusing his bile in smoke-rings and tantrums; in Amara's production—the first one that acquainted me with the play—the writer became more of convenient tool in the hands of the producer and he took on, by a turn of his 'doshala', both the role of an peon and boss with remarkable alacrity. Shyamanand himself playing the writer—with a grey-coloured buttoned-up tunic, showing a disconcerting punch—made no efforts to change physical appearance when he had to slip into the various roles of Peon, the Examiner, or the Boss. I dare say appearances matter—whatever the degree of naturalism projected.
>
> Mr Shyamanand on the other hand, as said above, had his production imaginatively designed. He froze his actors on the stage instead of letting them make due exists, which, when one comes to think of the play, studied admirably to the sameness that is there in persons of Amal/Bimal/Kamal. In the wedding scene, when the writer is underlying the inanities and its predictable platitudinousness, the girl instead of being shown in three different roles with Amal/Bimal/Kamal moves from one (the wedding night) to the other (to fight over his lazy morning habits) and then to the third (who is indifferent both to his son's illness and the ruined household), thus leaving the three tableau. With the last gestures frozen, it gives a new dimension to the play. Only, if the rough edges of these gestures are smoothed out, the production will improve four-fold.
>
> The set by Khaled Choudhury was an intrusion. It was neither aesthetically justified nor symbolically understandable. The only use the director made of it was to let Manasi and Mausi be played by the same girl (who gets into the scooped out triangular structure to say a few lines on a hidden mike). The director, however, also made use of the set to make effective stage pictures.

> One more notable feature of the production was the circular movements the director gave to his Amal/Bimal/Kamal, signifying, again very effectively, man's inescapability out of his viciously moving life-circle. There are scores of other inventive little things Mr Shyamanand had put in that one may like to write about. But when I personally didn't like was the loudness (the unsynchronized, loud music for one) that was underlined in all the roles. All the actors Amal (Vimal Lath), Bimal (Amar Gupta), Kamal (Arvindan) gimmicked quite a bit to encores. Indrajit (Kalyan Chatterji) was perhaps the weakest link. Diminutive as compared to Shyamanand, he shrieked away his presence to no particular effect. Also ineffective was Chetna Tiwari's Manasi. She was unable to bring out Manasi's conflict (as well as her helplessness in loving Indrajit). Shyamanand's own role of 'Lekhak' was quite inventive, full of changing moods and expressive variations, making use of his body and voice flexibly. To me, personally, it tended to be slightly overdone—the loudness of it, and the redundant gestures that he attached while reciting poetry whose meaning one gathered without his help anyway. Maybe he had in mind, as one got the hint afterwards, his uninitiated audience, but then it's misfortune that such a well-designed production had so many rough edges which could, no doubt, with a better rehearsed and a more pliable cast, be easily ironed out.

In its issue no. 40 (April 1970) the same journal *Enact* further reported:

> After successfully doing the rounds in Calcutta and Delhi, the Hindi version of Badal Sircar's *Evam Indrajit* landed in Bombay in March. A couple of years ago, the Gujarati adaptation, produced by INT, had flopped and in between there were sporadic productions of the original Bengali version and of Pratibha Agarwal's Hindi translation.
>
> So much has been written and discussed about *Evam Indrajit* that it would be redundant to go into its matter and content. However, since I belong to the school of thought (not yet satisfactorily challenged or disputed by any one) which questions the purpose of writing a play in India, in the middle 60's in a style, form and medium which was the rage in the fifties in Europe and America and which virtually became a spent force in the early sixties, I'll dwell for a little while on that point, before coming to the performance.

> Though the character teachings of the actor-author and of Indrajit are brilliant, the theme and content of the play are, by and large, a ragout of the works of Beckett, Adamov, Camus, Ionesco, Sartre and Vian an *olla podrida* [sic] that has been repeatedly chewed by serious-minded playgoers. The deeply pessimistic outlook and the state of metaphysical angst of humans, the bizarre objects, situations and images, the purposelessness of life, the disillusionment—all stocks-in-trade of French, British and American playwrights in the fifties—are paraded before the audience, a greater part of which is still steeped in age-old traditions and conventions that run counter to the surrealistic philosophy. Even the blending of the absurd with comedy and credibility—a compromise so effectively arrived at by Pinter and Ionesco earlier—and the constant allusion to Sisyphian labour—a pastiche of *The Myth of Sisyphus*—smack of an unimaginative emulation of the West.
>
> All this is not a detract from the playwright's theatrical expertise or his deep and sincere commitment nor is it a denigration of the non-conformist ideology. The pertinent question is: Are our novelists, playwrights and scenario writers devoid of originality that they are unable to produce something—an idea, an inspiration, a philosophy—novel and unique and that they should continue to be influenced by Western norms and thoughts?

Recalling the audience response, Jalan said: Our best audience and best response was at the show at Kalamandir, Calcutta, before Bengali audience. That gave us so strength because we were talking in Hindi and we had 100% Bengali audience and they responded to it.... The two other performances which come to mind were in Allahabad where the audience included professors, students and writers. In Kanpur the audience were diametrically different—an audience of shopkeepers. As a director, Jalan gives importance to the text and respects the dramatist. He tries to absorb the inner meaning at a deeper level, and plans production details in a limited way, allowing them to develop during rehearsals. If the writer is available, he holds long discussions to understand the authorial point of view. Jalan had regular consultations with Sircar while working on *Evam Indrajit,* thus establishing in practice the latter's opinion that his play had neither a happy nor a sorrowful ending.

Besides Pratibha Agarwal and Shyamanand Jalan, another theatre director, actor, screen writer who deserves accolades for raising the prestige of Badal Sircar to new heights in the annals of theatre production in India, in a language other than Bengali (not reckoning here the brilliant English translation of the play by the well-known theatre expert Girish Karnad), is Satyadev Dubey (1936-2011). As Satyadev Dubey himself states, he had his direct access to Sircar's text through Pratibha Agarwal's Hindi version. He reminisces,

> You cannot forget certain things that become so important in your life and one of these was the translation of *Evam Indrajit* that she sent me. And I loved it and I took her permission.... I don't think I ever paid her any royalty. In fact, later on, I made a rule that I'll not pay any royalty because I am going to do any commercial production, and if the playwright insists on his royalty, which is his right, I'll not do his play. But *Evam Indrajit* was such a discovery.... I feel so much in love with the play that despite the fact that I had done a lot of regular productions, odd productions, *Evam Indrajit* became an obsession—so much so that I could not imagine a production for years and years...and of course this also set me out in search of Manasi...till I suddenly realized that Manasi was just round the corner—Sulbha Deshpande! Why am I looking elsewhere?[13]

It is seldom that one genius (no matter what genre) considers the work of another genius a major integral part of his life. Satyadev Dubey assimilated Hindi version of *Evam Indrajit* with such a passion that this play became a part of his psyche and such a life-long obsession as nothing else. Satyadev Dubey says that every play he has done after directing *Evam Indrajit* has the shadow of this masterpiece on it.[14] Speaking at a round table discussion held in Kolkata in November 1996, Dubey interestingly stated that he was not interested in Badal Sircar (!), he was interested in no one except Satyadev Dubey, that is, his own self. Being interested in his own self, he considered his presence at the said round table discussion an opportunity of reexamining his own life and exploring his own past and that the play *Evam Indrajit* had been a major passion for him.

Explaining the impact of *Evam Indrajit* on the audience Satyadev Dubey later reminisced: "It was about the Indian reality as they knew it, it was a theatrically effective and crystallized projection of all the prevalent attitudes, vague feelings and undefined frustrations gnawing at the hearts of the educated urban middle class."[15]

Incidentally, when Satyadev Dubey came across a press report purporting to claim that Sircar had 'disowned' his earlier plays, including *Evam Indrajit*, he felt furious. For him it was something like denying his own entire existence and besides proving himself to be a bloody fool which he never thought he was. He expressed his thoughts in very simple language and very simple images.

> It was more like sort of having a brother and then being told that he was never your brother…so for a long time, Badal Babu and I were not on talking terms, for I could not forgive somebody when he had destroyed my life…for taking away something that was so much a part of my existence.… This was the sort of extreme, you can say, perverse attachment that I had with *Evam Indrajit.*[16]

Sircar, however, clarified that such misleading reports were the concoction of the press and that he had never rejected *Evam Indrajit* or *Baki Itihas*.

What Dubey stated further is still more significant and thought provoking. He stated: "Badal Babu means more than Shakespeare to me, means more than the Greek playwrights to me because he has been more a part of my life."[17]

Satyadev Dubey directed the staging of this play in 1970 by Theatre Unit, Bombay. Different roles were played by: Amarish Puri (Lekhak), Smt. Murdeswar (Masi), Sulva Deshpande (Manasi), Gaganan Bangera (Amal), B.A. Nayak (Bimal), Chandra Sekhar Sinha (Kamal), Satyadev Dubey (Indrajit) with assistance from Amol Palekar, Girish Ghosh, Ramesh Talukdar, R. Sindhe, Ashok Kulkarni, Uniati Palekar, Susama Pagenkar.

The Drama critic of *Enact* observed in its issue no. 64 (April 1972):

> Dubey's *Evam Indrajit* did not have as much sensitiveness of interpretation. He has given the Manasi-Indrajit such a focus in his presentation that the play acquired a very strong romantic colouring and all other characters became secondary. As a result, probably, he constantly used linear movements for Indrajit and Manasi and the unending circular motion emphasized by Amal-Bimal-Kamal, to bring out the repetitive and monotonous routine and mechanical existence, did not get enough importance. The inevitable pointlessness of all existence and consequent anguish of still being forced to live on, which was a major statement of the play, did not come across sharply enough. In this production even Lekhak became secondary

though he is the pivotal character in the play, holding together all the threads through his consent but frustrating search for some drama, or in other words the meaning, in life. Eventually, the play appeared to end rather tamely.

All the same the production otherwise had some very interesting and expressive moments; the long narrow platform across upstage was imaginatively used; the classical vocal music to mark out the Indrajit-Manasi sequences was often very evocative, though some variations on the same melodic base would probably make it more interesting. There was a pleasing simplicity in the total production which often brought the meaning with force and clarity.

Among the cast, Sulabha Deshpande most imaginatively brought out various aspects of Manasi with a wealth of characteristic detail. In contrast, Dubey himself as Indrajit was much more self-conscious and deliberate. His constant downcast eye and a coy romantic expression did not fit in with the restless adventurous character of indrajit. His voice also was feeble and lack sufficient projection, and his constant gesticulation was more distracting than articulate. But the most disappointing was Amrish Puri as Lekhak, who was rather colourless and inexpressive, in spite of his stature and deep voice. His rendering of the poems was particularly flat and lifeless. His indifferent acting went a long way in diffusing the center of the play.

Another critic observed:

Satyadev Dubey's splendid direction for the Theatre Unit helped a great deal in effectively projecting the various nuances of this slice of the 'Theatre of Dream', in keeping the brisk and uniform tempo and in providing an over-all aesthetic experience.

The performances of practically all the cast were good. Outstanding among them were two veterans, Amrish Puri as the playwright in search of characters and material and Sulabha Deshpande as Manasi, the heartthrob cousin-wife of Indrajit. Dubey himself in the role of Indrajit, the rebel who fails, came out with one of the finest performances of his career.[18]

Anamika's Production of *Evam Indrajit*

In 1976 the Hindi version of *Evam Indrajit* by Pratibha Agarwal was performed on 16 and 17 September at 'Tagore Theatre', Chandigarh, by the theatre group 'Abhinet' under the direction of Atulvir Arora. Atulvir Arora had been a product of the Department of Hindi of the Panjab University, Chandigarh, where another theatre, artist Mohan Rakesh was also a student. Apart from his interest in theatre, Atulvir Arora had also been a dedicated researcher and prepared a dissertation on the topic "The Hindi Novel of Today in the Context of Modernism". A clip from the production is appended to the present writing. The individuals who played various roles in the production came from spheres of life as different as civil engineering, electrical engineering, zoology, metallurgy, mechanical engineering or from the teaching faculty. Different roles were played by Harish Bhatia (Lekhak), Inder Prabha (Mausi), Aloka Mehndiratta (Mansi), Ashok Kochar (Amal), Vijay Mathur (Vimal), Madhav Singh (Kamal) and Deven Joshi (Indrajit).

In the brochure issued by the organizers, Deven Joshi wrote:

> *Evam Indrajit* depicts the adventures of an alienated self in the realms of psyche, soul, cosmos, permanence, a quest for meaning in this futile existence that knows no end; a journey through the dark alleys of chaos where rules—didactic and shameless as they are—dictate our lives. Here is portrayed one disintegrated and disillusioned Indrajit, a split atom for whom things fall apart, centre cannot hold.
>
> Indrajit as he emerges in the denouement is the creation of his own thought and aspirations. Birth and death are no events for him for the vast promising span in between—life—is luminous with the resplendent rays of his optimism, the world that opened innumerable possibilities was to be treated upon till death would come not as a means to escape but as something satiating to mark the completion of an episode. But no! the waxen wings of Icarus melted the moment he tried to overreach himself and down he fell on the rocky surface of defeat where 'dead' tree gives no shadow and cricket no relief....
>
> Badal Sircar, hence, has waged a war against the notions nurtured blindly by society. Life is absurd for man is pinned by what he wants to overcome. He merely wriggles –calls it movement and in his bovine complacency compromises with regimentation. The finer instincts of life—faith, hope, and love—are adulterated by the insipid products of human intellect. Man is a mere robot computerized in this age of reason. But is that all? Is this monotony the alter of Moloch where all are to be sacrificed? No! Badal Sircar calls for the negation of this gloom. There may be many Indrajits who, in spite of their best efforts find life confronted with a big question-mark. The disillusionment should not defy the idea of life or movement itself. The son of God suffered as there is a perpetual permanence in the act of suffering. The agony of Sisyphus—the torture of Prometheus

> stand in majestic splendour amidst the chaos of life. There is no question of comfort or despair; the question is of confrontation.[19]

During May 1968 another theatre group 'Amra' also performed *Evam Indrajit* in Hindi in Delhi. This production gave an impression of simplicity, restraint and economy, seemingly conceived as a narrative.

It may also be of interest to learn here that a Marathi translation of *Evam Indrajit* by Shrikant Kulkarni published in December 1997 also made Pratibha Agarwal's Hindi version as its source.

A scene from *Evam Indrajit* in Hindi, Translator: Pratibha Agarwal, Group: Abhinete, Chandigarh Director: Atulveer Arora.

A scene from *Evam Indrajit* in Hindi, Abhiskar, Mumbai.

The impact of *Evam Indrajit* was so great that a young college student Narasimhan while directing the play in Mysore, did not use stage light at all, wrote B.V. Karanth on a Kannada production of *Evam Indrajit*. The play referred to here was performed in the college courtyard with the lights from the classrooms serving as the background.

The play *Evam Indrajit* was also performed under the direction of Mushtaq Kak (with Anoop Trivedi and Naveen Thakur as music directors) at the main auditorium of the Sri Ram Centre, Delhi from 15 to 16 September 2003.

It may not be out of place to record here that Badal Sircar's *Evam Indrajit* is not only taught at the under-graduate, post-graduate level of different universities of India but also prescribed in the syllabus of Civil Service Examination conducted by West Bengal Public Service Commission.

Notes and References

1. *Bohurupee,* Kolkata, July issue 1965.
2. *Enact* (New Delhi), 59, November 1971: 69—report by Sumanta Banerjee under the title "Playwright in Perspective".
3. *Ibid.*, 66.
4. *Enact* 59, November 1971: 72—report by Satyadev Dubey under the title "Sircar and Indian Theatre".
5. Satyadev Dubey, 'Introduction' to Badal Sircar's *Evam Indrajit* translated by Girish Karnad. Kolkata, 1974: iv.
6. http://mohanmaharishi.in/productions/evamindrajit.php
7. *Enact* 16, April 1968—report by A.J.
8. *Ibid.*
9. Pratibha Agarwal's article "Hindi Anubade Badal Sircarer: Natak O Manchayan" [Badal Sircar's plays as translated and produced in Hindi] *Bohurupee Journal*, Kolkata. No. 117. May 2012: 266.
10. Badal Sircar's *Evam Indrajit,* tr. Pratibha Agarwal. New Delhi: Rajkamal Prakashan, 1969. Price: ₹ 3.75 Subsequent imprint available is dated 2014, as published in Rajkamal Paperbacks.
11. *Op. cit.*
12. *Contemporary Indian Theatre, Interview with Playwrights and Directors.* Ed. Rajinder Paul. Sangeet Natak Akademi, Hope India Publications, New Delhi, 2006: 74.

13. Plays in a National Perspective: Round-Table Discussion I A Synoptic Report Calcutta, 28-30 November 1996. Bharatiya Bhasha Parishad Conference Room published on the occasion of Badal Utsava (16-19 July 2009): 5. Natya Shodh Sansthan, EE-8 Sector II, Bidhan Nagar, Kolkata–700091.
14. http: //www.newsclick.in/india/outsider-badal-Sircar-1925-2011. Accessed on 07.02.2015 Kolkata.
15. Satyadev Dubey, 'Introduction' to Badal Sircar's *Evam Indrajit* translated by Girish Karnad. Kolkata, 1974: iv.
16. *Op. cit.*
17. *Op. cit.*, 6.
18. Adi F. Doctor's report in *Enact* April 1970 No. 40.
19. Brochure published by the theatre group.

[The research has been sponsored by the Visva-Bharati and UGC under the Research Award Schemes approval No. F.G-115/2012 (HRP) dated 05-09-2012 and F. 30-1/2014/RA-2014-16-SC-WES-5369 (SA–II) dated 20-02-2015.]

□

The River as a Self-Reflective Veiled Spiritual Protagonist in Hermann Hesse's *Siddhartha*

Roger Augustine

Siddhartha the ninth novel of Herman Hesse originally written in German in a simple and lyrical style in the year 1922 drew world-wide and enormous attention of the English reading public after the English version was rendered by Hilda Rosner in 1951. Hesse's travel to India in 1910 facilitated in making this compact lyrical work an allegory about the finding of wisdom. It gives rendition to the mysticism of the writer and gradual attainment of the spiritual enlightenment in a pure Indian philosophical context. The name Siddhartha comes from two Sanskrit words "Siddha" meaning "achieved" and "Artha" meaning "what was searched for". Thus Siddhartha is "he who has found meaning (of existence) or goals". The story is set in a place of ancient India during the time of Gautama Buddha. The entire novel deals with the spiritual journey and the self-discovery of an ordinary man. A major preoccupation of Hesse in writing *Siddhartha* was to cure his own 'sickness with life' by immersing himself in Indian spiritual philosophy and mysticism. The novel shows the profound influence and deep spiritual knowledge of the *Upanishads* and the *Bhagavad Gita* and is structured on three of the traditional stages of Hindu life such as student (*brahmacharin*), householder (*grihastha*) and recluse (*vanaprastha*). The First Part of the novel having four chapters and the Second Part with eight chapters correspond respectively, to the Four Noble Truths and the Noble Eightfold Path of Buddha making a total of twelve chapters in the novel. It is also interesting to note the significance of the number twelve for Hesse, the son of a Christian clergy, who had the full knowledge of the importance of 'Twelve' in Christian theology and Jewish tradition, as it is the complete, perfect and divine number.

A mature eco-depth sensitivity coupled with a deep psycho-spiritual awakening that unfolds the Indian Mysticism is the preoccupation of Hesse in the novel from the outset. The harmonious awakening and balanced growth in three realms, namely ecological, psychological and spiritual, are essential for a person to attain enlightenment: an eco-psycho-spiritual awakening leading to enlightenment. The romantic characteristic is an undeniable feature vividly seen in the novel *Siddhartha*. The novel opens with this high note of romanticism. Siddhartha is the son of a Brahman who grows up carefree in the perfect harmony of nature and under the care of his parents. The nature imagery in the beginning of the novel is striking:

> In the shade of the house, in the sunshine of the riverbank near the boats, in the shade of the Sal-wood forest, in the shade of the fig tree is where Siddhartha grew up, the handsome son of the Brahman, the young falcon, together with his friend Govinda, son of a Brahman. The sun tanned his light shoulders by the banks of the river when bathing, performing the sacred ablutions, the sacred offerings. In the mango grove, shade poured into his black eyes, when playing as a boy, when his mother sang, when the sacred offerings were made, when his father, the scholar, taught him, when the wise men talked. (9)

Nature and the people were benevolent to him indeed. He grew up as the apple of their eyes in the lap of nature enjoying unlimited affection and care of the people. However, the young mind growing in the harmony of nature was in a state of dilemma and complete restlessness. To quote the novelist:

> He found no delight in himself. Walking the rosy paths of the fig tree garden, sitting in the bluish shade of the grove of contemplation, washing his limbs daily in the bath of repentance, sacrificing in the dim shade of the mango forest, his gestures of perfect decency, everyone's love and joy, he still lacked all joy in his heart. Dreams and restless thoughts came into his mind, flowing from the water of the river, sparkling from the stars of the night, melting from the beams of the sun, dreams came to him and a restlessness of the soul, fuming from the sacrifices, breathing forth from the verses of the Rig-Veda, being infused into him, drop by drop, from the teachings of the old Brahmans. (11)

Further, the romantic sensibility encrusted with eco-depth sensitivity is fervently elucidated in a high poetical and imaginative note, narrating the inner disposition of Siddhartha. Here one is undoubtedly reminded of the Wordsworthian treatment of nature. Hesse writes:

> He learned something new on every step of his path. He saw the sun rising over the mountains with their forests and setting over the distant beach with its palm trees. At night he saw the stars in the sky in their fixed positions and the crescent of the moon floating like a boat in the blue. He saw trees, stars, animals, clouds, rainbows, rocks, herbs, flowers, stream and river, the glistening dew in the bushes in the morning, distant high mountains which were blue and pale. Birds sang and bees buzzed, the wind whispered through the rice-field. All of this, a thousand-fold and colourful, had always been there, always the sun and the moon had shone, always rivers had roared and bees had buzzed, but in former times all of this had been nothing more to Siddhartha than a fleeting, deceptive veil before his eyes, looked upon in distrust, destined to be penetrated and destroyed by thought, since it was not the essential existence, since this essence lay beyond, on the other side of the visible. (49-50)

Hesse, here not only applied romantic colour to the description of nature but also enumerates the internal change taking place within Siddhartha. Thus the path to knowledge, awakening and the saga of metamorphosis of Siddhartha is highlighted by the author through the flamboyant description of nature. Again,

> Beautiful were the moon and the stars, beautiful was the stream and the banks, the forest and the rocks, the goat and the gold-beetle, the flower and the butterfly. Beautiful and lovely it was, thus to walk through the world, thus childlike, thus awakened, thus open to what is near, thus without distrust. Differently the sun burnt the head, differently the shade of the forest cooled him down, differently the stream and the cistern, the pumpkin and the banana tasted. (50)

The striking descriptions of nature and the imagery created not only make the poet highly romantic in his approach, but also helps the readers to have a bird's eye view of the things waiting to happen in the young life of Siddhartha where he is going to be led by the worldly lures and earthly loves as is evident from the following:

> Short were the days, short the nights, every hour sped swiftly away like a sail on the sea, and under the sail was a ship full of treasures, full of joy. Siddhartha saw a group of apes moving through the high canopy of the forest, high in the branches, and heard their savage, greedy song. Siddhartha saw a male sheep following a female one and mating with her. In a lake of reeds, he saw the pike hungrily hunting for its dinner; and propelling themselves away from it, in fear, wriggling and sparkling, the young fish jumped in droves out of the water; "the scent of strength and passion came forcefully out of the hasty eddies of the water, which the pike stirred up, impetuously hunting" (50). "All of this had always existed, and he had not seen it; he had not been with it. Now he was with it, he was part of it. Light and shadow ran through his eyes, stars and moon ran through his heart. (50)

With an insight of the 'spirituality of emptiness' of soul and mind, and with a sole elevated goal to become fully 'empty, empty of thirst, of wishing, of dreams, of joy and sorrow' (20), Siddhartha decided to leave behind his home to become an ascetic, a wandering beggar of Samanas in the hope of gaining spiritual illumination. Govinda, a true follower and the best friend of Siddhartha also joins him and fasts, becomes homeless, renounces all personal possessions, indulging in intense meditation. Embracing the path of Samanas for the sake of blissfulness along with Govinda, Siddhartha was able to cultivate deep sensitivity to the 'atman-knowledge'. This mysticism is revealed in the following way:

> There is, Oh my friend, just one knowledge, this is everywhere, this is Atman, this is within me and within you and within every creature. (25)

The life of Samanas could not provide Siddhartha what he longed for. His soul remained thirsty and he was fully dissatisfied. It only made him completely restless. Here Siddhartha dares to leave the path of Samanas too. Thus, he says to his dear friend Govinda:

> Soon, Govinda, your friend will leave the path of the Samanas, he has walked along your side for so long. I'm suffering of thirst, Oh Govinda, and on this long path of a Samana, my thirst has remained as strong as ever. (25)

In pursuit of spiritual illumination and wisdom, Siddhartha and Govinda meet Lord Buddha, the holy exalted one having attained enlightenment.

In conversation with Gautama both Siddhartha and Govinda acknowledge the elegance and the depth of Buddha's teachings. Govinda hastily and happily joins Buddha's order. But the restless Siddhartha soon comes to a realization after listening to his "wondrous teachings" that no one can impart teaching of enlightenment. He later realized that it is purely a personal effort and subjective. The subjectivity of the spiritual liberation or enlightenment also is the theme of the novel. This is an eternal truth which Siddhartha found only at the end of all his pursuits, which, with no doubt, he suspected as a young man. Siddhartha says to Govinda his friend:

> Wisdom cannot be passed on. Wisdom which a wise man tries to pass on to someone always sounds like foolishness. Knowledge can be conveyed, but not wisdom. It can be found, it can be lived, it is possible to be carried by it, miracles can be performed with it, but it cannot be expressed in words and taught. (141-42)

Therefore he plans to leave his friend and the "last teacher who had appeared on his path, even him, the highest and wisest teacher, the most holy one" (42). Siddhartha is of the opinion that the individual seeks an absolutely unique and personal meaning that cannot be ever presented by a teacher and he thus resolves to carry on his quest alone. This is the kind of mysticism Hesse brings into the novel.

In the novel, 'River' plays a pivotal role that grooms the destiny of Siddhartha. Throughout the two parts of the novel the 'River' appears repeatedly with remarkable importance. The nature description is vivid and emphatic in many of the chapters along with the detailed treatment of the river. The young Siddhartha seeks, finds and learns meaning of life and achieves spiritual awakening from the river. The flamboyant river becomes a medium for Siddhartha to face strange situations, people and things in life nourishing him with many spiritual experiences of enlightenment.

The pursuit of Siddhartha drew him near the hut of a ferryman by the river. The first encounter of Siddhartha with ferryman is unique and unforgettable. The river and the ferryman later became inseparable from and inevitable in his life. It was by the riverside Siddhartha met his real guide and teacher. Being tired after a long journey and reaching at night by the river Siddhartha fell asleep and had a strange dream. As he woke up:

> The pale river shimmered through the door of the hut and in the forest, the dark call of an owl resounded deeply and pleasantly. (52)

The next morning Siddhartha begins the journey with the ferryman. He was taken up by the beauty of the river as "the wide water (was) shimmering reddishly in the light of the morning" (52). It is here that the great significance of the river in the life of ferryman is revealed. These words become revelations for Siddhartha and are the center of the novel.

> It is a beautiful river, I love it more than anything. Often I have listened to it, often I have looked into its eyes, and always I have learned from it. Much can be learned from a river. (53)

The conversation between Siddhartha and Vasudeva, the ferryman unfolds that the river has taught Vasudeva great lessons. The river becomes a witness of the meeting of Siddhartha with the ferryman and the departure he makes later. The departure from the river was a deviation in the life of Siddhartha to lead a life of worldly lust, "though without being a part of it". If so, the returning to the river also meant a coming back to the spiritual path and an awakening. While leaving the river and the generous ferryman Vasudeva, whom Siddhartha is unable to pay, he assured that he would return to the river later to compensate him in some way. To this Vasudeva replies:

> Surely, I have learned from the river. Everything comes back! You too, Samana, will come back. Now farewell! (53)

The departure from the river was a beginning of worldly life of attractions and affections, wealth and lust for Siddhartha. As soon as Siddhartha moves away from the river, he meets Kamala, a beautiful woman, a courtesan of affluent men in whom he is highly interested. However, Kamala urges him to become wealthy in order to win her affections so that she might teach him the art of love. Siddhartha though despised worldly possessions as a Samana, agrees to Kamala's suggestions. In the pursuit of wealth, he becomes an employee of Kamaswami, a local businessman, as suggested by Kamala, and insists that he should allow Kamaswami to treat him as an equal and not as a subordinate. Siddhartha easily succeeds in this attempt due to the qualities of patience and tranquility that he learned to practice as an ascetic as contrasted with Kamaswami's fits of passion. Later, however, wealth and lust prove too much for Siddhartha. He develops anxiety, self-hatred, and indulges in gambling. Eventually Siddhartha becomes Kamala's lover, only to realize later the emptiness of luxurious lifestyle he had chosen and the resultant vacuum of the spiritual fulfillment created in his heart:

> There is a path in front of you, you are destined for, the gods are awaiting you (85). Go on! Go on! You are called upon!

One morning, overwhelmed by his own depression and disconcerting dreams, Siddhartha walks out of his fancy home and never returns. He undergoes a series of changes and realizations. Once again he reached the large beautiful river in the forest, the same river where he had met the ferryman Vasudeva. He felt that the life he had lived until then was over and done with. Hesse expresses the feeling of disgust in Siddhartha in the following words:

> Dead was the singing bird, he had dreamt of period. Dead was the bird in his heart. Deeply, he had been entangled in Sansara, he had sucked up disgust and death from all sides into his body, like a sponge sucks up water until it is full. (88)

Truly, the river was a *Guru,* a teacher formerly for Vasudeva and later for Siddhartha. It is said by Siddhartha at the end of the novel.

> Vasudeva was taught by river. He had noticed that the river spoke to him, he learned from it, it educated and taught him, the river seemed to be a god to him, for many years he did not know that every wind, every cloud, every bird, every beetle was just as divine and knows just as much and can teach just as much as the worshipped river…he knew everything...only because he had believed in the river. (147)

The river becomes a mirror for Siddhartha where he sees reflected his own true image. It acts like a storehouse from where the spiritual messages are given to him at the appropriate time. In the chapter entitled 'By the River', the river becomes the central point in most of the events, the deep silent but most powerful witness for many things happening in the novel. It is the point of the meetings and departures. Siddhartha reaches back to the same large river, weakened with tiredness and hunger, having no goals, as said:

> There was nothing left but the deep, painful yearning to shake off this whole desolate dream, to spit out this stale wine, to put an end to this miserable and shameful life. (89)

He leaned against the trunk of a coconut tree bent over the bank of the river, and embraced it with one arm and looked down into the running water only to be filled with the wish to let go and drown in the waters. Apparently, the river exhibits to him the shallowness of his soul,

> A frightening emptiness was reflected back at him by the water answering to the terrible emptiness in his soul. (89)

When Siddhartha stared into the water, the river reflected his distorted face and he only spat at it. Having lost all hope and no goal left, he let himself fall straight down to drown and die."Things are going downhill with you" he said to himself and looked at the river and saw the "river too going downhill, always moving downhill, and singing and being happy through it all." He liked this well and smiled at the river (97). The chapter concludes with an urge for transformation that the river brought into him. There with a cheerful heart he looks into the rushing river and felt renewed:

> Never before had he liked water so well as this one, never before had he perceived the voice and the parable of the moving water thus strongly and beautifully. It seemed to him, as if the river had something special to tell him, something he did not know yet, which was still awaiting him.... The new Siddhartha felt a deep love for this rushing water and decided for himself, not to leave too soon. (101)

The river witnesses yet another strange meeting, of Siddhartha with Govinda, his childhood friend, whom he left years before, though, there takes place a separation soon between them Govinda, who is passing through the area as a wandering Buddhist, leaves him. But Siddhartha decides to spend the rest of his life in the presence of the 'spiritually inspirational river'.

The chapter "The Ferryman" commences with a yearning of Siddhartha to stay beside the river. As Siddhartha was looking at the water, he saw that the river too was looking at him. This prefigures the spiritual unification, of *atman* and *Brahman*, 'becoming-one-with', or 'God-with-man'. This is the mysticism of Hesse. In this the author shows *atman* looking at *Brahman* and *Brahman* looking at *atman*.

> Tenderly he looked into the rushing water, into the transparent green, into the crystal lines of its designs, so rich in secrets. He saw bright pearls rising from the deep, quiet bubbles of air floating on the surface, reflecting the blue of the sky in it. With a thousand eyes the river looked at him, with green ones, with white ones, with crystal ones, with sky blue ones. (103)

In becoming one with the river he was feeling grateful, and learning to love the water. Here Siddhartha hears a newly awaking voice telling him,

"Love this water! Stay near it! Learn from it" and he decided to learn from it and listen to it. He realizes that if he understood this water and the secrets of it, then "would also understand many other things, many secrets, all secrets" (102). Here Siddhartha learned a great lesson that touched his soul, "The water ran and ran, incessantly it ran, and was nevertheless always there, was always and at all times the same, and yet new in every moment!" (103). This chapter records yet another meeting of Siddhartha with the old ferryman, Vasudeva, who ferried him over two decades ago. At the end of the long conversation they recognized each other. Vasudeva listened keenly to all what Siddhartha said, as the river had taught him to do so, and allowed every word of Siddhartha to enter his mind. Finally Vasudeva claims:

> It is as I thought. The river has spoken to you. It is your friend as well, it speaks to you as well. (106)

Siddhartha with a grateful heart acknowledges and comments on Vasudeva's great virtue of listening and longs to learn this art and virtue from him which he himself had learned from the river. But Vasudeva urges him to learn it from the river itself:

> You will learn it, but not from me. The river has taught me to listen, from it you will learn it as well. It knows everything, the river, everything can be learned from it. (106)

After many days of staying by the riverside for listening and learning, Siddhartha grasps another truth from the river which Vasudeva had already done. He learns that the river is everywhere and has only present time in it. This is the divine attribute of God, *Brahman*: He is Omni-present and in him only the flow of the eternal present exists. The Jewish and the Christian theology define God as "I am" that shows the presence of the present time. In the words of Hesse:

> The river is everywhere at once, at the source and at the mouth, at the waterfall, at the ferry, at the rapids, in the sea, in the mountains, everywhere at once, and that there is only the present time for it, not the shadow of the past, not the shadow of the future. (108)

Siddhartha learns a great truth from here that his life too is a flowing river which had passed through stages of boyhood and then manhood, and his previous births, his death and the final return to Brahman, all is in the present. "Nothing was, nothing will be, everything is, everything has existence and is present" (108).

The river never ceased to teach Siddhartha many things as he was always eager to listen to it. During the rainy season when the river was full with the increased flow of the water and made a powerful noise, he realized that the river has many voices. The river is the voice comprising all voices of nature. It is the 'voice of the many voices' and possesses very many voices. "...the voice of a king, and of the warrior, and of a bull, and of a bird of the night, and of a woman giving birth, and of a sighing man and a thousand voices more" (109). Vasudeva agrees with him saying "all voices of the creatures are in its voice" (109). Here Siddhartha too hears a sound, a word, a syllable, the beginning and the end of all prayers of the Brahmans, "Om". He realizes that this is the summit of all voices, the one voice echoing all voices, and that is 'Om' the eternal sound that stands for Brahman. The river thus reverberates 'Om' which represents *Brahman.* The holy word that he heard by the riverside, roughly means "that which is perfection" or "completion". It prefigured an end and a beginning; end of an entangled life in *Sansara* and beginning of a new life of enlightenment. This brings to mind the Hegelian philosophy which speaks of the process of everything in the world claiming that every end is a new beginning. As the sound of "Om" reached his ears, the dormant spirit woke up realizing the foolishness of his actions. It was by this riverside he comes back to life, knowing about the status of his life. The river showed him his distorted face clearer than a crystal clear mirror and the water begins to wash him completely to make him purer than the purity of snow symbolizing God as the final purifier,

> And again he knew about Brahman, knew about the indestructibility of life, knew about all that is divine, which he had forgotten. (90-91)

Here again for a second time, Siddhartha falls into a deep sleep at the riverside but without dreams. As he woke up, he felt weightless and chainless: the heavy weight of worldly life was no more in his soul and the fetters of entanglement broken, and he had completely abandoned the previous life. He came to his senses under the coconut tree by the riverside, with the holy word "Om" on his lips, and then fell asleep, woke up, observing the world as a new man.

> When 'Om' entered his consciousness, he became aware of himself in his misery and in his error. (90)

The resounding sound of 'Om' from the river which pierced the depth of his soul led Siddhartha towards spiritual purification. By the riverside,

"Siddhartha was nevertheless transformed, was renewed, was strangely well rested, strangely awake, joyful and curious" (92). Obviously, the river is seen as *Brahman* that purified and transformed Siddhartha. It is this nature of Brahman in the river which teaches the whole humanity truth about life. The river which had the great symphony of a thousand voices actually consisted of a single word, Om: the perfection.

While many years passed by, Siddhartha and Vasudeva lived by the riverside, there came a group of monks, the followers of Gautama, the Buddha, to be ferried across the river. They had come to get back to their great teacher Gautama as he was sick and "would soon die his last human death to become one with salvation". His old beloved Kamala came with her little son (Siddhartha's son) travelling by the river to pay the last visit to Gautama in whose teachings she had taken refuge after Siddhartha had left her. As the pilgrims were getting close to Vasudeva, to be ferried across, they heard a wailing scream of a woman, Kamala, whose face had suddenly grown pale as she had been bitten by a small black snake. Siddhartha and Vasudeva rescued her by carrying the collapsed Kamala and the little boy to their hut, washed the wound and made her drink some healing potion. Regaining her consciousness for a short time, she recognized her old beloved Siddhartha pointing towards her little boy saying that he was Siddhartha's son. Kamala kept on looking at him till he saw the life fading from her eyes gradually. For a long time he sat looking at her peacefully dead face. Siddhartha went outside and sat the whole night before the hut, listening to the river. On the following day Siddhartha told Vasudeva:

> I sat here (whole night), I was listening to the river. A lot it has told me, deeply it has filled me with the healing thought, with the thought of oneness. (116)

The river made him to experience suffering though no sadness had entered his heart. After Kamala's death, Siddhartha composes himself and takes care of the resistant boy until the child flees away. Although Siddhartha is eager to find his run-away son, Vasudeva advises him to let the boy find his own path, much like Siddhartha did himself in his youth. Vasudeva makes him understand human nature and differentiates the status of the boy from his own:

> Water wants to join water, youth wants to join youth, your son is not in the place where he can prosper. You too should ask the river, you too should listen to it. (120)

As Siddhartha looked into the water, there came many images associated with suffering, before him in the moving water, first his father, lonely, mourning for his son; then he himself, alone, yearning for his distant son; then there appeared his son too, lonely as well, greedily rushing along the burning course of his young wishes. In the words of Siddhartha:

> Each one heading for his goal, each one obsessed by the goal, each one suffering. The river sang with a voice of suffering, longingly it sang, longingly, it flowed towards its goal, lamentingly its voice sang. (135)

Listening to the river with Vasudeva, Siddhartha realizes that time is an illusion and that all of his feelings and experiences, even those of suffering, are part of a great and ultimately jubilant fellowship of all things connected in the cyclical unity of nature. The ferryman Vasudeva always had an answer for all questions: "Ask the river about it, my friend." Living beside the river, listening to the many voices of the river and finding answers to all queries became the lifestyle of Siddhartha. He learned valuable lessons of "waiting, patience and listening" from the river.

> He sat lost in thought and waited. This he had learned by the river. This one thing: waiting, having patience, listening attentively. And he sat and listened to his heart, beating tiredly and sadly, waited for a voice. Many an hour he crouched, listening.... (128)

> (Siddhartha was) nothing but a listener, completely concentrated on listening, completely felt, that he had now finished learning to listen. (136)

Vasudeva understands that Siddhartha had reached the moment of illumination and great realization after many lessons from the river and therefore, his role became insignificant at this juncture. He feels that his work is done and now he must depart into the woods, leaving Siddhartha peacefully fulfilled and alone once more. Because he knew that 'the vessel emptied was fully-filled', Siddhartha is taught everything by the river.

Sometime later, Govinda heard about an enlightened ferryman at the river and travelled to meet him, not initially recognizing him as his old childhood friend Siddhartha. Govinda asks old Siddhartha to share his wisdom to which Siddhartha replies that for every true statement there is an opposite one that is also true; that language and the confines of time lead people to adhere to one fixed belief that does not account for the fullness of the truth. Because nature works in a self-sustaining cycle, every entity carries in it the potential for its opposite and so the world must always be considered complete. He confesses at the end that he has learned several lessons from the river, all he had to do was, to listen and the river taught him many lessons: "Most of all, I have learned here from this river" (142).

The enlightenment for Buddha beneath the Bo tree (in the novel and historically too) is the same for Siddhartha beside the river. Everyone who listened to the river learned impeccable lessons for spiritual life. Initially in the novel, Vasudeva, learned from the river and attained spiritual perfection, and gradually Siddhartha achieved his enlightenment listening to the sounds of the river that gave long-lasting peace. It led to the essence of his journey and eventually Govinda, the friend, also is shown the path of enlightenment with the special spiritual allusions to the river. Ralph Freedman who wrote the biography *Hermann Hesse: Pilgrim of Crisis* mentions how Hesse commented in a letter "[my] Siddhartha does not, in the end, learn true wisdom from any teacher, but from a river". The river's pivotal role in the making of enlightened Siddhartha is matchless and the importance is more than of a real character in the novel. It no more appears to be any symbolic character but the real spiritual character, the protagonist that framed, formed and enlightened Siddhartha. From time immemorial the concept of fire in Hindu philosophy is highly spiritual and the *Sanaatanadharma* teaches that the ever burning fire by consuming burns away all impure and unholy things in the world yet remains holy and pure throughout. This spiritual notion is overlapped in the novel by the mention of the ever flowing river that has the spiritual quality of transforming and paving the way for spiritual enlightenment. The river, thus, in the novel helps Siddhartha to accomplish what his name suggests, "the one who has achieved what he has searched for" and therefore it is unmistakably assumed that the river makes possible the metamorphosis of Siddhartha and the final spiritual acclamation in Indian mysticism "*aham Brahmaasmi*" ("I am Brahman").

Work Cited

Hesse, Herman. *Siddhartha* (Translated version) (Noida: Maple Press Pvt. Ltd., 2012 edition).

□

Search into History: Nayantara Sahgal's *Rich Like Us*

Shahaji V. Gaikwad

Creative Indian English writers of the postcolonial times turned to their nation's history for subject matters. They have got the store and made creative use of it in their novels. The novelists like Salman Rushdie, Khushwant Singh, Anita Desai and Nayantara Sahgal deal with the past showing its relevance with the present. These writers see the relationship between the past and the present and they have made characteristic use of it in their writings. Sahgal's *Rich Like Us* presents India's past through the past of her characters. The protagonist Sonali's past intermingles with the nation's past and *vice versa.* In the narrative of the novel she digs out her own past which surprisingly turns out the nation's past. Her first person narration focuses on her search into history. The present paper thus is an attempt to examine Sonali's search into history and the motive behind it.

The novel's locale is New Delhi and the time is one month after the declaration of the Emergency in the nation. The Emergency plays a stimulus for Sonali's search into the past of the nation. She appears as a woman who believes in individual's freedom, particularly the freedom of women. At Oxford she has imbibed liberal values which are unknown in her country. During her stay in England she comes to know what freedom is and what is meant to be free. She practically enjoys it with her friend Ravi Kachru, a Kashmiri Hindu. She commits herself to the ideology of freedom so much that allegiance to any other ideology seems enslavement to her. She rejects Marxist ideology ignoring her friend Ravi's insistence to do so. Sonali does not want to follow any doctrine because it may not as good as the doctrine of freedom. Being a woman she knows what is subjugation which men have no experience of. Men can enjoy all sorts of freedom including the freedom of choice of doctrine. Ravi can commit to any doctrine because, Sonali says:

> ...he was a man. He had never fought a battle of freedom, never been patted down firmly when his sap was rising, never had sari trotting his legs, making in the wind and running to catch a bus a threat to life and limb, never had his mother set up a howl when he went and got a haircut. He had no idea what the simplest subjugation were all about. I, who did, had no intention of chaining myself to any doctrine when I had just lost some of my chains. (Sahgal 123-24)

This is one of reminiscences of Sonali that conveys what Dennis Walder calls "a gendered search for freedom" (109). But the novel is not all about the gender issue; it is about the loss of individual's freedom in the Emergency.

The Emergency has its evil effect on Sonali who has lost her job in the civil service. Jobless Sonali has enough time to devote to her reminiscences. She turns to her past when she joined the civil service as an idealist who had belief in nation's 'self-reliance' policy. The young class of the civil servants dreamed of India's bright future after its Independence. Sonali believes that her professional class has "a new tradition to create...independent worth to prove" (Sahgal 22). The line between the bureaucrats and the politicians is drawn as the civil servants start to think them as "we" and politicians as "they". Yet it is thought that both classes are two different sides of the same coin. They stick to an idealism and hold a view that they are bound by more than a discipline. They firmly believe that their job is to stay free of the political circle. Sonali acts on the idealism and beliefs and questions the legal side of the arrangement between Neuman and Dev. The former is willing to invest in Dev's soft-drink factory by an arrangement which Sonali thinks is breaking of the nation's self-reliance policy. She takes move to oppose the mutual arrangement between Dev and Neuman and this move causes to lose her job.

For Sonali it is not simply losing one's job but it is losing one's freedom to do job, to work. She knows that the Emergency is not need-based since no other priorities are mentioned; even it is not unexpected happening. Her civil servant class do not see the Emergency as she does; they do not speak against it and thus are involved in "the conspiracy of silence" (24). Even the people in India blindly accept what they are given without any thought to it. Sonali says that the people in India accept the repressive regime because "we are blind from birth, born of parents blind from birth. We do not see what we do not want to, and when we cannot avoid a nasty sight it still can't do much to hurt us" (24).

Sonali notes how the people call the PM, who declares the Emergency, "many armed goddess" and how she with her father and son forms "a regular Holy Trinity" (196) to them. This populism, in which symbols are used, appeals people and fulfills their need of incarnation of god in the present. It is seen in Nishi's reaction to the Emergency; to her it is an order brought on chaos.

Nishi sees how the Emergency has made the country comfortable; before it the country had been in "a mess, people screaming for more wages or bonus, or just screaming, too many political parties, so humiliating to explain to foreigners" (87). People feel secure in the Emergency and they—teachers, lawyers, school-children—go in delegations to congratulate the PM for the gift of the Emergency. Only Sonali can see the motive behind it; to her it is the beginning of dictatorship and end of democracy which allows people their freedom. When all-around her conform to the new system, she feels like an outsider opposing it. She sees a similarity between her and her father; both feel as outsiders. Her father was a Maharashtrian who married to a Kashmiri woman; he is an outsider in the Kashmiri atmosphere. Sonali is sympathetic of her father and wants to know about his childhood and family. She also wants to know about his place and:

> ...a plateau history about guerilla warfare in harsh boulder-strewn terrain, table-topped hills with jutting triangular peaks, ideal for hill fortresses and their defense, and Shivaji, that match-for the Moghuls who had so brilliantly defended them against Aurangzeb's elephantic armies. (145)

This reminiscence by Sonali is her search into history; it is the history of Maratha. Her search into history becomes important in context of the Emergency. Shivaji fought against the mighty Moghuls for 'Swaraj'—people's rule—using tactics of guerilla warfare. Shivaji stands for motivation to resist and his war tactics the means to resist. History teaches Sonali that a minority group of people can fight with mighty power.

Sonali searches her father's papers, letters, playbills and personal and official correspondence in order "to reconstruct segments" (145) of his life. During her search she finds a printed circular issued by Sir Frederick Puckle, Secretary to the Government of India, on 17 July 1942. At the bottom of the circular a newspaper clipping displaying Mahatma Gandhi's comment is pinned. There Gandhi says that "Let the masses know that there are many other ways of earning a living than betraying the national interest" (146). Sonali's father, who was a civil servant then, underlined these words with a red pencil showing his interest in them. However her father never showed his allegiance to Gandhi and Quit India Movement openly when he was in service. Sonali realizes that her father was a divided man whose "body had served the sovereign power and his heart and mind, *satyagraha*" (145). Sonali states the condition of her father that how he "remained on the seesaw all his working life till Independence" (146).

Sonali's father stands opposite of the present civil servant class which conforms to the oppressive rule. Her father was scared of the British rule but in his heart and mind he loved freedom. This is the reason why he came out "with the energy of a whole, not a divided man" (186) after the country got freedom. Sonali's act of searching her father's past is an act of reconstructing the nation's history. In her reminiscence of her father in chapter thirteen Sonali recalls how he once said that India's history was without the "split atom" because "We were Not Guilty of Hiroshima, Nagasaki, or sending Jews in cattle cars to gas ovens. We could afford to remind ourselves of a past others were trying to forget. And we joined ours seamlessly to the present" (186). Sonali observes that Indian history is history of progress. It is continued during the enormous changes like cultivators are made landowners while *Zemindari* is abolished, Maharajas ruled are ruled out, and Indian products are promoted.

In recalling history the protagonist Sonali reconstructs the nation's history. She sees the Prime Minister Shastri's agenda of removal of poverty as an attempt to continue history-as-progress. But the Emergency has changed the concept of history-as-progress giving it "new twists and turns" (26). In such a period as this a nation's history may be revised and twisted. Sonali's father is afraid that "history would be revised and re-written" because all "dictators meddled with history" (199). During the Emergency attempts are made to revise history in the form that suits the ruler. A part of attempts to revise history is seen in posing the Prime Minister as "many-armed goddess" (191). Ironically, Sonali's father, who knows how dictatorship works, fails to advise his daughter to resign from the civil service post. Sonali thinks that he could have told her that "When the Constitution becomes null and void by the act of a dictator, and the armour of a modern state confronts you, *satyagrah* is the only way to keep your self-respect" (198).

Lessons from history help Sonali to prepare herself to face the Emergency alone. From it she learns the means to maintain the self-respect.

In addition to this she gains from history the knowledge of the making of British India and the painful memory of her great-grandmother's 'sati' act. Sonali comes to know from the manuscript that her great-grandfather was against the 'sati' practice and he supported the Britishers' attempt to abolish it. He was of the view that "the abolition must be absolute" (147). He was in favour to reform Hinduism while urging "a clean sweep of the cruel and corrupt practices that were making a mockery of true religion. The burning of widows was the most barbarous of this" (149). Sonali tells how her great-grandfather the historical sati practice and the effects of the law. In his debate with his British friend Mr. Timmons, the great-grandfather says that the sati act of seven ranis of a raja was an act of murder by those who forced them to do it. Mr. Timmons says that the British Government could not interfere in this barbarous act because it was not British territory.

Sonali's grandfather wrote that "Mr. Timmons' view of history was that it had happened" and "it had become inevitable" (151). Timmons' view of history is more detached because he is an outsider. He looks at it from a colonizer's perspective. But Sonali's great-grandfather opposes this view of history. He says that what had happened "need never have happened at all if people had behaved differently at the time" (151). He wished the British Government to act with responsibility and interfere in the sati practice. He concludes that the English are not different from Portuguese and Dutch who are crude conquerors and are indifferent to sati practice. The rulers leave the sati issue to time to end. They think that the sati practice will not survive with time as useful and rational learning advances. The people like the great-grandfather support some changes and also expect a gradual progress toward self-government.

The search into the past brings Sonali a painful memory of her great-grandmother's sati act in her husband's funeral pyre. The event turns out as a revelation about her grandfather who as a boy tried to save his mother from the burning pyre. He dashes forward to the pyre but he is stopped by two men. The boy wants to kill those men because they are murderer of his mother. He wants equal justice in this case: murder for murder. This move of the boy inspires Sonali to save mother India from the burning pyre of the Emergency. The event of his mother burning into the fire was traumatic to the boy. The past chases him even in his adulthood. A painting in an art gallery of England reminds him of the actual event of his mother burning in the fire. He sees that the painting "has all the hallmarks of the particular, as some moment in history recaptured" (166). The devious familiarity of the scene makes the grandfather visualize it:

> A procession of them took her from the house, past familiar scenery, knowing where they were her. They helped to climb the funeral pyre, bedded down solicitously on the stacked wood where so lately her husband's corpse had lain, and then stepped back to a great safe distance as the flames leapt up, to watch her dance with death. (170)

This reconstruct of the past shows a dimension of Indian history: it is barbarous. The sati practice is the black spot in India's history. It is the most heinous act that caused innocent deaths in British India. It creates empty space in the lives of those children, younger or elder, who are deprived of their mother. This scene form the past no doubt brings illumination to Sonali. She realizes that we cannot be passive towards cruelty and depravity; it does not matter whether we children or adults. She writes:

> On a narrow parapet enclosing a funeral pyre I saw a boy of nineteen balancing dangerously, unconscious of the danger to himself, as he fought savagely to kill his mother's murderers. Not all of us are passive before cruelty and depravity. He had not been. (171)

It is a lesson to those who are rulers. Sonali's search into the past is oriented to collect the examples that show the resistance to the oppressive power. She sees it in the struggle of the boy in Connaught Place to escape from the police and in Rose's beggar's slipping from his tormentor's grasp. Such examples of resistance will fill in Sonali the courage to stand against the Emergency. Her search into the past is intended to comment on the present. She addresses "the present through the past" (Walder 112). Her first person narration facilitates Sonali to view the past form her own perspective and thus offer comment on the present. Knowledge of history helps Sonali to see how the life of ordinary people like Rose is affected by the new rule. She sees that Rose has lost those qualities in her which make her optimistic. Rose "seemed to have lost her natural verve and bounce" (Sahgal 252), Sonali observes.

The Emergency has affected the lives of ordinary people like Rose. The present government is as barbarous as Turkish dictators who once ruled Delhi. This association is suggested in Sonali's observation on the way back from Rose:

> The long drive out to see her and back, past the Qutab Minar, built when Turkish tribesmen were Sultans of Delhi, gave plenty to think

> about and helped to explain why she had that quenched look. It's what happens to ordinary life when power is arbitrary, as power always has been on this prize of Gangestic plain.... (252)

Rose has lost enthusiasm for life as the new government comes into power. The gentle form of democracy is replaced by the arbitrary power, the Emergency. It is like Turkish dictatorship that kills the zest for life. It also affected Sonali's father who desired to escape it through death. Sonali herself has lost hope of change in the present rule—the Emergency. She is pessimistic of such a miracle. Sonali reveals her mind to upper-class English Marcella who asks Sonali to accept the job of research assistant till the Emergency is over and then she can take another one:

> "And after all it needn't be a lifelong commitment," said Marcella gaily. "If you find you don't enjoy it, you can always do something else later, when the Emergency is over."
>
> "Over?"
>
> A word can start the rumour of a rainbow. Until she said it I hadn't realized the Emergency could ever be over, or that my future hadn't come to an end on a steamy day in July this year. (299)

Under this pessimistic reaction to Marcella's comment lies Sonali's view of history as a kind of permanent subsoil beneath the present (Walder 107-08).

Sonali accepts the job of research assistant because she loves research in history. She comes home, after she has food with Marcella and her husband, and takes "a book of history off...shelves, opened it and started to read" (299). She reads from history that India in seventeenth century "presented an impressive picture to the world and created the modern legend of wealth and power" (300). On the next page, she reads that "a great power existed in India embracing a developed civilization with great attainment in letters and the arts, with polished manners and complicated social life" (300). These selective pieces from history are deliberated quoted in order to mark the change in the present. Sonali's emersion in the past is her preparation for the future. "Immersed in the past, I was preparing all the while for the future..." (301), Sonali writes. Sonali's takes up research in history because it is a worthwhile activity; however, Neuman gives it up because he thinks it as financially worthless activity. Neuman once was greatly fascinated with knowledge of history; he was "tempted...by a fragment from the past, some wonderous bit of broken stone, or a jewel of temple" (3). But now he thinks that his knowledge if history has "fallen into disuse" because it "did not contribute to the financial basis of his happiness" (3).

Neuman's approach to history is detached and utilitarian. History does not affect him now as it does to Sonali. The emergency does not make any impression on him because he sees it from detached perspective. It doesn't matter to him who rules if bureaucracies are made easier to handle. To Sonali study of history is a preparation for future. She searches into history to find some solution to the present time. Seen from this perspective the text of *Rich Like Us* becomes Sonali's research into history. Although the novel's time-span is four months beginning with July 1975 till the first Deewali in the Emergence, the flashback takes us into history of the Persians, the Moguls, the British Empire and the rise of Indian nationalism, Civil Disobedience Movement, the demand for Muslim state to events leading to June 1975. This is the history that Sonali searches into. A study of history helps Sonali to see the extent to which the democratic ideals are weakened in the Emergency. Sonali—the spokesman to Sahgal—thinks that research into history is the only worthwhile activity to counter the Emergency. To her friend Rose history provides one with wisdom. Rose has a sense of history. On the other side, her step-son Dev is clean of history. Rose thinks that Dev is "a lunatic…cut off from continuity before and behind" (177). Sonali reaps the benefits of research into history. She comes out with certain findings of research.

One of the findings of Sonali's search into the past is that the lies about women's deaths have been told in the past as well in the present. The barbarous behaviour of men towards women is still seen in the present. The deaths of women in the past were actually the murders of women by the society but the truth was never told. There are so many examples that can be told to support this statement. The present is no exception to this; people tell lies about the deaths of women in the present too. Rose's death is a murder by her stepson Dev but he has told the people that she has fallen into the well due to her over drunkenness. Indian history is the history of lies about deaths of women and it is still continued in the present. Sonali notes that "Here in the house the revision of history has begun and there would be no end to lies" (285). The great-grandmother was forced to burn on the pyre hence it was a murder but it was called sati—a sacrifice for the husband by his wife. No regime, the past as well as the present, ever cared for women who formed a half of the society then and now. This finding of Sonali's research opens the feministic discourse in the novel.

Works Cited

Sahgal, Nayantara. *Rich Like Us*. New Delhi: HarperCollins Publishers, 2003.

Walder, Dennis. *Post-Colonial Literatures in English: History, Language, Theory*. India: Blackwell Publishers Ltd., 2002.

□

STATEMENT ABOUT OWNERSHIP AND OTHER PARTICULARS OF

The Atlantic Literary Review

FORM IV

(See Rule 8)

Place of Publication	:	New Delhi
Periodicity of the Publication	:	Quarterly
Printer's Name	:	Manish Kumar
Nationality	:	Indian
Address	:	B-2, Vishal Enclave New Delhi 110027
Publisher's Name	:	Manish Kumar
Nationality	:	Indian
Address	:	B-2, Vishal Enclave New Delhi 110027
Editor's Name	:	Sunita Sinha
Nationality	:	Indian
Address	:	402, Rameshwaram Apartment, Miss Mandal Compound, East Boring Canal Road, Patna, Bihar
Names and addresses of individuals who own the newspaper and partners or shareholders holding more than one per cent of the total capital	:	K.R. Gupta B-2, Vishal Enclave New Delhi 110027

I, Manish Kumar, hereby declare that the particulars given above are true to the best of my knowledge and belief.

Sd/-

Date: 01st July, 2015

MANISH KUMAR
Publisher

Listening to the Wild: Deep Ecology in David Malouf's *An Imaginary Life*

Sharmistha Chatterjee (Sriwastav)

Kathy my sister with the torn heart,
I don't know how to thank you
For your dreamtime stories of joy and grief.
Written on paper bark.
You were one of the dark children
I wasn't allowed to play with-
Riverbank campers, the wrong colour
(I couldn't turn you white)
So it was late I met you,
Late I began to know
They hadn't told me the land I loved was taken out of your hands.
[*Two Dreamtimes* written for Oodgeroo Noonunccal by Judith Wright]

A large part of the Australian postcolonial writing has come from the whites like Judith Wright, A.D. Hope or David Malouf who have consciously tried to champion the indigenous culture and environment of the aborigines. Their writings display a deliberate effort to adapt to and appreciate the tradition of the natives, which they had failed to do erstwhile as outsiders or whites, who had shared their time between the developed countries (like UK or USA) and Australia which is their second home.

For modern Europeans, or even Asians, it is probably difficult to understand the native Australian concept of 'Dreamtime' which talks of a period when Ancestral Beings shaped the land, creating all species and human beings. These beings are thought to live eternally in spirit form. But more importantly 'Dreamtime' believes that Human beings are a part of nature, closely associated with all other living things. There is also a blurring of the distinction between past and present and time is seen and conceived as eternity.

Retrieval of the aboriginal tradition in Australian literature therefore essentially includes invocation of pristine and primitive forms of nature and indigenous practices such as corroborees, using, wooden boomerangs or even shamanism which formed a part of the 'Dreamtime'. Terry Gifford would describe such an attempt as post-pastoral which emphasizes on the need to identify certain distinctive qualities of nature and culture and be brought into dialogues, if they offer the signs of a rightful and just way forward. According to Gifford: "Long time survival of our species will necessitate newly refined values and relationship in spatial terms-that is, how we relate to land in its organic forms and process. In this, our inner nature might have to attune better to the lessons evident in outer nature." Gifford considers ecopoetry [ecological writing] as a cultural tool of attunement and in his words:

> Older than writing, the practices of ecopoetry has always performed this function of attunement in many cultures globally, often in the form of songs. In Western literature ecopoetry took the form of the personal tradition of poetry. Its neglect and decline has been a feature of the industrial–technological colonization of the planet's resources that has led to the present environmental crisis. (75)

While such attempts to negotiate with primitive culture and nature is clearly visible in Australian ecopoetry, literary ventures of other types remain unexplored and less appreciated. David Malouf's *An Imaginary Life* [1978] is a case in the point. Largely allegorical and poignantly lyrical, the novella defies straightjacketed categorization. What stands out clear from Malouf's treatment of Ovid's exile and his subsequent encounter with the feral boy of the wilderness are that, Malouf did not mean the work to be an example of a historical novel. More an allegory and a journey to self-discovery, Malouf's Ovid is the white colon in contact with the aborigine [the feral boy and also Ryzak and his family and such an encounter paves the way for the possibility of a retrospection of civilized normative standards and re-evaluation of what one may call the *savage.*

Sriparna Dutta feels:

> Malouf never denies the existence of the alien Australia—the Australia of the Aboriginals. White Australia may try to erase the Aboriginals from their consciousness but it is only through an acceptance of this 'other' Australia—that the second or third generation whites can find their true identity, and solve the problem of identity. (105)

Malouf himself says in the afterword of the book: "Ovid is very much an actor, inclined to exaggerate for effect, so very little of what he tells us is reliable. I have used his poem of exile, "Tristan", for my picture of Tomis and have drawn on Book III of "Fasti", his study of the chief Roman Festivals, for details of the Parilia. My hint of the Scythian graves is in Herodotus" (154). Although, Malouf adheres to the historical details of the death of Ovid's brother one year older than himself, in early youth, and the later exile of the poet to the remote island of Tomis, because he had offended the Emperor Augustus, his purpose was, in his own words: "To make this glib fabulist of 'the changes' live out in reality what had been, in this previous existence merely the occasion for dazzling literary display" (156).

The encounter of Ovid with the child which forms the main part of the book, according to the author, has no basis in fact, but Malouf has taken the pains to crosscheck with the best account of such a phenomenon. J.M.G. Itard's painstaking observations of Victor the wild the boy of Aveyron, which no writer on the subject can ignore. More important is probably Itard's preoccupation with the problems of innate and learned experience which Malouf deals with at greater lengths in this book *An Imaginary Life*.

It is here, that there is a need to intercept and interrogate as readers, the possible meaning and vision of life and nation that Malouf wants to project in his work. While the Renaissance reader would find Ovid as the most modern of the Latin poets, the most worldly and accessible, the most human, an epitome of civilized grace and sophistication, it is also true that the poet had his skepticism balanced with the love of the fabulous, the excessive. It is this love of the fabulous, the strange and the wild that begins the process of learning and unlearning in close communion with nature. *An Imaginary Life* thus becomes a rethinking of the concepts of 'nature' and 'nurture'.

Malouf's Tomis is not the ancient historical port. It is a village consisting of a hundred huts made of woven branches and mud, with roofs of thatch and floors of beaten mud covered with rushes and in this village Ovid is forced, during his exile to live a life of basics. "Each hut has a walled yard and a byre where the animals can be brought in and stalled for the winter. Above the byre in one large room, we sleep and in the winter on wooden benches above a layer of snow. Burning peat. In summer the rest of the house is opened up and I have a room of my own, with a low table for writing and a paillasse of clean straw.... My life here has been stripped to the simplest terms" (8).

It is the civilized Ovid who is the least person in the village community, "a crazy, comic old man grotesque, tearful, who understands nothing, can say nothing, and whose ways, so it must seem to this dour people are absurdly out of keeping with the facts of our daily existence" (9). The condition of Ovid approximates the Ulysses of Tennyson who 'mete(s) and dole(s) unequal laws unto a savage race,' or as Lisa Hill suggests, Ovid is the alter ego of Malouf, who explores the themes of intellectual isolation, conformity and the bleakness of some cultures influenced by his ten-year sojourn in Europe and return to Australia in 1968.[1]

It is interesting that Ovid refuses to call the natives 'Uncivil', yet his despair is evident because no one in Tomis speaks his tongue and he is initially isolated from the world of men as if he belonged to another species. At night he suffers from the horrible nightmare of digging, finding his own grave along with the wolves. The poet's state of abject desperation can only be changed once he feels the need: "Now I too must be transformed" (26). Peter Morton suggests:

> Malouf finds deep possibilities in the theme of exile—there are the obvious allusions to the convict experience but also to the way in which the fate of the exiled poet torn between, Rome And Tomis, becomes a powerful analogy for the complex fate of an antipodean writer of European reflexes and ancestry to feel exiled wherever he happens to be: "equally in Australia or from Australia." Ovid's nostalgic lectures about the Italian countryside and how these new alien vistas of the edge must be seized and mythologized by the imagination has an equally obvious relevance: Malouf is truly Australian postmodern Romantic not least in his implicit promotion of an attitude to a 'new' Tomian/Australian landscape which, as Hills has put it, 'requires the dissolution of the European self in order to establish a new self'. (16)

The search for the new self begins when Ovid comes into contact with the child—"It is a child" as the old man explains: "a boy of ten or so, a wild boy, who lives with the deer" (40). Even before the boy has been found by Ovid and the hunters there is a significant dream: "We have all been transformed, the whole group of us, and become part of the woods. We are mushrooms, we are stones—I recognize my companions. I am a pool of water. I feel myself warm in the sunlight, liquid, filled with the blue of the sky; but I am the mere a broken fragment of it and I feel, softly the cloud passing through me.... A deer.... It takes a part of me into itself, but I do not feel diminished.... I break in circles" (55-56).

It is this extraordinary dream that propels Ovid to understand and begin a new lesson of initiation into the heart of nature. As the ice inside him cracks, he reaches out to encompass the bio-centric universe where he unlearns his 'anthropocentric' conception of the trees, and the birds. This is what the 'radical' environmentalists would label as a wilderness movement called 'Deep Ecology'. This dates its origins into an essay published in 1972 by the Norwegian Arne Naess, who called for environmentalists to embrace an ethic, termed 'biospheric egalitarianism' that would place humans on more or less equal footing with other species. Recast in philosophical terms, this can be stated as the distinction between anthropocentricism, the belief that humans stand apart and above the rest of creation, and biocentrism, which rejects a human-centred perspective by looking at history from the perspective of other species and nature as a whole.

Ramchandra Guha, in *Environmentalism: A Global History*_quotes the eight principles offered by Arne Naess to unite deep ecologists [version 1993]. Among them, there are a few which uncannily match with David Malouf's approach to wilderness, richness and diversity of life forms on earth, forms human culture, and human being's (read civilized Ovid's) position in relation to this environment. The relevant principals are:

> Richness and diversity of life forms on earth, including human culture, have intrinsic worth.
>
> The flourishing of human and non-human living beings has intrinsic worth.
>
> The worth of non-human beings is independent of their usefulness for human purposes.
>
> Present human interference with the non-human world is excessive, and the situation is worsening.
>
> Humans have no right to reduce this richness and diversity, except to satisfy vital needs. (85)

Replete with criticism, which accuses deep ecology of misanthropy and a peculiar blindness of its own which ignores environment degradation outside the wild and the human suffering that is its consequence, the movement nevertheless is an eye opener to the interdependence of human beings and the wild and nature [wild] as a sustainer, motivator and energizer. The term *wild* thus,

> has emerged in environmental criticism as a distinctive aesthetic/ ecological and moral category.... The term stresses that element of anything that is resistant to human control, prediction or understanding, 'the unmanaged energy of nature' (Mabey) manifest in even the densest cities in the weeds that push through small cracks in the pavement or fissures in the wall.... (qtd. Clark 33)

Ovid Publius Naso's first vision of the feral boy in the wilderness of Tomis strangely motivates him to become sturdy and strong again and in his own words he "(has) stopped mooning about and regretting my fate". He increasingly finds solace in nature—the brushwood, the animals and insects, the sea, the fish and the smooth black pebble which according to him have been "created perfectly after their own needs", every detail of their anatomy useful, necessary, and for that reason admirable, even when they are a product of terror "and more importantly" Ovid says he has "stopped finding fault with creation and (has) learned to accept it" (58) Ovid's assertion probably best explains Naess' principle that non-human do exist in their own right.

The old man Ryzak and his family [Lullo, the grandchild, his mother and Ryzak's mother] find a place in the poets heart and he is filled with wonder and appreciation of the native customs manners and even their language.

> He is the closest friend I have ever had.... He has taught me to weave a net—there are different sorts of nets, and traps also, for the different kinds of fish—I am happy to learn all this. What is beautiful is the way one thing is fitted perfectly to another.... (58-59)

About the native language which Ovid slowly picks up, he says "It is not at all like our Roman tongue, whose endings are designed to express difference, the smallest nuances of thought and feeling. This language is equally expressive, but what it presents is the raw life and unity of things" (59).

Murali Sivaramakrishnan in his essay posits the following challenge:

> If the world of abstractions that Language encompasses is nothing but a collection of socially constructed texts (in sense of woven fabric) and contexts, then the possibilities of encountering the world outside the human mind in its entirety becomes an intellectual

> impossibility and the human being collapses within his/her own prison house of language!" and yet, he says, citing a perceptive ecocritic, 'language might have trapped us into the cultural constructions of our environment but there is a real world outside which continues to be wounded and harassed critically!' So then, among the post enlightenment problematic, the trajectory of theorizing in the world has led us directly to engage with physical nature outside the text, and it was a natural extension of the theoretical debate! The text spills over to the globe! (Intro, 7)

Ovid's attempt to appreciate the 'other'—their culture, language and to understand the intrinsic unity of things not only allegorically establishes Naess principles but also is an answer to Sivaramakrishnan's challenge, and also [what already has been explained] the rhetoric of post-pastoral, where the colon rediscovers the native heritage.

Two things simultaneously happen—(1) It is Ovid the civilized who beings to accept Ryzak and his village—thus reiterating the *post-pastoral* and (2) The feral child is caught "wolf boy, godling satyr—is alive" and "The village has accepted him within its walls." Thus reiterating the "principles of deep ecology."

Malouf gives Ovid extensive space whereby he weighs his childhood, its simplicity and moves towards discovering his manhood which makes him realize that: "The simplicity of those early years at Sulmo fitted so ill with my new role as man about town, as sophisticated poet of the metropolis that I should have felt only anxiety and some sense of disgust if I tried to reconcile the two" (18).

Yet it is the same poet who takes off his sandals to be with the boy [the boy goes barefoot and they wade through the rushes to a turfy island. Importantly, the poet tries to teach the child to speak, as if one could make the child of the wilderness a human being and what makes a human one is his ability to communicate in speech (Language)]. This he does partly because of his desire to talk,—to talk in his civilized tongue which would set him apart from the savages, but in the process, the child draws the poet into his consciousness: "It is his sphere of knowledge, a kind of library of forms that he has observed and committed to memory, another language whose hieroglyphs he can interpret and read" (89). The boy assumes the role of teacher pointing out to the poet the tracks in the grass and explaining with signs and gestures of his body which bird or beast it is, that has made them. This probably promotes 'new cultural ethic of the wild' made up of four normative claims: (1) The necessity of commitment to the potentialities and limitations of place; (2) The belief in the wild and its processes as the best teacher for humanity; (3) The identification of the wild with the sacred; and (4) The use of the wild as a guide for the diverse, inclusive, participatory, democracy.[2]

Suellen Campbell, quotes Arne Naess:

> Organisms are knots in the bio spherical net or field of intrinsic relations [qtd. in Tobias 39]. Theory and ecology agree that there's no such thing as "self-enclosed, private piece of property, neither a deer, nor a person, nor a text nor a piece of land."

Campbell further argues:

> Perhaps the most important idea that follows from this premise is that human beings are no larger the center of value or meaning. The best examples of this new belief in theory may be Foucault's argument (at the end of The Order of Things) that the concept of 'man' as we generally understand it—of individual human as centers of intelligence and spirit and therefore value in the world—is historical one that is now disappearing. (133)

For both poststructuralism and deep ecology the assumptions underlying "humanism" have become untenable; we need new ways, they (which) agree to understand our place in the world. It is this what makes Malouf's Ovid take a decision: "The language I shall teach the child is the language of these people I have come among and not after all my own" and he also decides, "I shall never go back to Rome". Ovid can ultimately discover his true identity only by embracing the life with the boy in the wilderness and even beyond Tomis—"Now you will become at last the one you intended to be" (90-91). And herein begins the final metamorphosis where he realizes that the old self must be driven out to let the universe in.

> According to theory, and here Lacan is important, we emerge from the unity of infancy only when we bring to experience ourselves, as separate from everything else, especially from our mother's bodies. This happens the moment we enter into the network of language. The "symbolic order" that will determine what we become. At the core of our sense of self, then, is our feeling of loss and desire for the unity born of loss. Loss makes us what we are and desire is an empty force...which drives us but can never be satisfied.

Ecologists also seen an experience of lost unity and a desire to regain it as central to our human nature (qtd. in Campbell 134)

Ovid, then moves towards this desire for the unity born out of loss and blur the line between colonized and the colon. For the Australian landscape, where the exiled Whites had settled themselves to establish a colony, Ovid's renunciation (of sophistication, to be initiated into a life of simplicity and subsequent unity of with nature) approximates the regard of the whites for the natives and a re-appraisal of the aboriginal environment and tradition.

Notes

1. For details please refer to the website of Peter Morton, and the article on *An Imaginary Life*, entitled, *Evasive Precision: Problems of Historicity in David Malouf's An Imaginary Life. https://sites.google.com/site/petermortonswebsite/home/articles/malouf-s-an-imaginary-life* and, *http://anzlitlovers.com/2011/03/22/an-imaginary-life-by-david-malouf/* Posted by: Lisa Hill | March 22, 2011, *An Imaginary Life*, by David Malouf.
2. For new cultural ethics of the wild please refer to, "Wilderness" in *Ecocriticism* by Greg Garrard. Oxfordshire: Routledge, 2004.

Works Cited

Primary Source

Malouf, David. *An Imaginary Life*. London: Vintage Books, 1978.

All the quotations from the text refer to the above edition.

Secondary Sources

Campbell, Suellen. "The Land and the Language of Desire: Where Deep Ecology and Post-Structuralism Meet." *The Ecocriticism Reader: Landmarks in Literary Ecology*. Ed. Cheryll Glotfelty and Harold Fromm. Athens: University of Georgia Press, 1996.

Clark, Timothy. *The Cambridge Introduction to Literature and Environment*. New York: Cambridge University Press, 2011.

Dutta, Sriparna. "David Malouf's Exploration of the Problem of Identity: A Reading of Remembering Babylon" in *Australian Literature: Identity, Representation and Belonging*. Ed. Jaydeep Sarangi. New Delhi: Sarup & Sons, 2006.

Gifford, Terry. "Judith Wright's Poetry and the turn to the Post-Pastoral." *Ecological Humanities* ISSUE 48, MAY 2010 Australian Humanities Review.

Guha, Ramachandra. *Environmentalism: A Global History*. United States: Longman, 2000.

Sivaramakrishnan, Murali and Jana, Ujjwal. ed. "Introduction", *Ecological Criticism for Our Times: Literature, Nature and Critical Inquiry*. New Delhi: Authors Press, 2011.

□

The Ordinary and the Extraordinary Aspect of Hemingway's Code Heroes: An Overview

Smita Jha

There is perhaps great substance and meaningfulness in the statement that "no other author of our time has had such a general and lasting influence on the generation which grew up between the world wars as Ernest Hemingway" (Lania 1961). Hemingway's case as a writer is highly interesting for several reasons. The first of these reasons is that it is difficult to separate Hemingway the man from Hemingway the writer because most of his writings, in one way or another, relate directly to his personal life. Secondly, Hemingway the writer has, in a striking way, his own bearing upon Hemingway the man, for right from his early age he was determined to be a writer. Thirdly, Hemingway was so much a man of enterprise and action, of daring and adventure that in his very lifetime he grew into a legend. And, lastly, we have to keep wondering as to how Hemingway, who spent so much of his time over other pursuits and activities, could be able to write poems, plays, short stories and novels. As such, it would be proper and profitable to keep in view all these aspects of his colorful personality in order to be able to undertake an assessment not only of his writings in general but also of his code characters in particular.

Ernest Hemingway, we all know, was rather a prolific writer; in fact, he had so shaped himself as to lose no opportunity to render his impressions and experiences into an articulate form. His first book entitled *Three Stories and Ten Poems* was published in 1923, and it was immediately followed by a collection of his stories called *In Our Time* in 1924. Two years later, that is, in 1926 Hemingway brought out two of his novels, the satirical short novel, *Torrents of Spring* and *The Sun Also Rises*. At this point we cannot do without recalling that *The Sun Also Rises* achieved immediate success and was indeed acclaimed as great work of fiction. His second volume of short stories, *Men Without Women*, was published in 1927, and it was followed two years later by his second novel entitled *A Farewell to Arms*. In 1932 Hemingway brought out a book about bull-fighting named *Death in the Afternoon*, while the third volume of his short stories entitled *Winner Take Nothing* came out in 1933. He wrote a travelogue called *Green Hills of Africa* in 1935, while shortly thereafter he wrote two of his powerful short stories, *The Short Happy Life of Francis Macomber* and *the Snows of Kilimanjaro*, that emerged out of his experiences of prolonged hunting in Africa. The year 1936 saw the publication of his next novel, *To Have and Have Not*. Hemingway's play, relating to the Spanish Civil War, captioned *The Fifth Column* came out in 1937. From 1940 to 1952 Hemingway wrote three novels named *For Whom the Bells Tolls* (1940), *Across the River and into The Trees* (1950) and *The Old Man and the Sea* (1952). It did not come to the world as a surprise that he received the Nobel Prize for literature in 1954. And equally so, there was nothing unusual about his shooting himself to death in 1961. *A Moveable Feast*, brought out posthumously in 1964, contains essays concerning Hemingway's years in Paris from 1921 to 1926.

It is generally said that Ernest Hemingway was not merely a rebellious, an aggressive individual but also a manly writer, tough and virile, and that he may be looked upon as perhaps the manliest among twentieth-century writers. Somehow or other, Ernest Hemingway the man forced his way into growing as Ernest Hemingway the legend, a legend in his very lifetime. However, in order to be able to understand and appreciate the real nature of his character, we have to examine the very course of his life in all its fullness and diversity. Although he had been born in a well-to-do middle-class family at Oak Park in Illinois, right from his childhood he was a victim of emotional tension arising out of the conflict between "the Spartan demands of his physician father" (Fenton 1954) and "the rich artistic aura which his mother attempted to cast over her family" (Fenton 1954). All the same, there were the grains of precarious wisdom in Hemingway. During his stay at the Oak Park school, it is true, he was interested as much in sports and outdoor activities as in acquiring learning; nevertheless, even as a boy his zeal for writing was stimulated both by the nature of the school curriculum, with its emphasis on classical myths, narrative poems and novels, and by the particular gifts of two of his teachers, Miss Biggs and Miss Dixon.

Before we undertake a study of the code characters in Ernest Hemingway's major novels, it is but proper that we try to understand and explain the implications of the term 'code character'. It is generally thought that Ernest Hemingway's characters are delinquents, drunkards, sexual maniac or perverts, extroverts and outdoor people, that they are, more or less, in the nature of social outcastes, frivolous, cynical and rootless, and that they are the people who look upon life as cheap, exciting, sensational, briefly enjoyable sport, and not as serious, sustained or meaningful business. Not unnaturally, it is said that "the brutality of the Hemingway fiction world has led many readers to think of the authors as a kind of caveman of literature" (Wegenknecht 1969). However, as we go through Hemingway's writings, we find that his case is not as simple as it has been made out to be. It is indeed true that, in certain ways and to a large extent, Hemingway's female characters, in spite of their quaintnesses and oddities, are far simpler than their male counterparts, for without much hesitation or deliberation, we may place them in three distinct categories: (a) those whose lives are the least complicated and who, with certain qualifications, represent a sort of ideal womanhood, such as Catherine Barkley in *A Farewell to Arms,* Maria in *For Whom the Bell Tolls*, and Renata in *Across the River and into the Trees*; (b) those who are predatory sex-maniacs and have nearly dehumanized themselves, for example, Brett Ashley in *The Sun Also Rises* and Margot Macomber in *The Short Happy Life of Francis Macomber*; (c) and those who appear as benevolent mother-figures, such as Pilar in *For Whom the Bell Tolls* and Marie in *To Have and Have Not*. And though it is also true that Hemingway's women are the victims of terrible situations, yet his major male characters, his protagonists are far more complex than his female figures.

Hemingway's major male figures may be, and are generally, divided into two groups: (a) the Hemingway hero; (b) and the code hero. Earl Rovit calls the former the 'tyro' (Rovit 1963) and the latter the 'tutor' (Rovit 1963).

The Hemingway hero is usually a young man who, despite physical and emotional injuries, tries almost incessantly to learn to live in a world that is pervaded by uncertainties, anxieteties, violence and chaos. This is the post-First World War world which has seen the utter collapse of all traditional values and in which sensitive individuals feel confused and bewildered and lost. In view of the obtaining situation there is naturally very little scope for personal initiative and heroism in such a world, and there is naturally very little opportunity for an exercise of options against high stakes in the prevailing condition. It certainly goes to Hemingway's credit that in spite of his intense awareness of all adverse factors, or perhaps because of it, he succeeds in creating characters who face the problems as best as they could and who assert themselves as well as they could in the face of big obstacles in a world of stark barbarism. No doubt, Hemingway's heroes, such as Nick Adams in *In Our Time*, Jack Barnes in *The Sun Also Rises*, Frederic Henry in *A Farewell to Arms*, Robert Jordan in *For Whom the Bell Tolls* and Richard Cantwell in *Across the River and Into the Trees,* are the victims of one sort or another, and yet their uniqueness lies contained in the fact that, in their own peculiar and extraordinary ways, they make sincere efforts to evolve a code of values that would guide and sustain them in the course of their lives. Nick Adam is the son of a doctor; Jake Barnes is a journalist; Frederic Henry, a student of architecture, is an army Lieutenant, while Robert Jordan, a teacher of Spanish at an American college, fights in Spain. They exploit their own limited and meager resources to give a direction and a meaning to their lives. However, the milieu, the surrounding they find themselves in, does not permit them to function as they would like to. Endurance, perhaps, occupies the topmost place in the hierarchy of their values. They do also attach great importance to a code of personal ethics, according to which they respect fellow sufferers, refuse to betray them, and demonstrate courage in the face of danger or death.

These heroes are honest and virile young people, but also sensitive; they are outdoor men with a flair for adventure, but also nervous. They are in a state of trepidation because they have seen people being wounded or killed, bloody bodies being disfigured beyond recognition, Caesarian operations being performed without anesthesia, helmets full of oozing-out brains, and evil in its most brutal and undisguised form. Many of them have had a similar kind of childhood. They do experience a kind of void within them, but they do not betray either their feeling of fear or their feeling of vacancy. They have realized that personal relationships are extremely fragile in nature and that trying to look for permanence in human relation is to court nothing but disappointment. They have a mortal fear of loneliness, for it tends to crush them under its burden. As such, they cultivate and develop an interest in outdoor life, and take to rituals, the rituals of bull-fighting, of deep-sea fishing, of big-game hunting. It is true that they have seen nothingness at the centre of the world and that they are in despair; nevertheless, they are not desperate, for with the help of their code they have learnt to come to some sort of peace with this nothingness.

Most of the Hemingway heroes are homeless, rootless people, exiles and expatriates, who have moved away from their native culture. And they are exiles not merely literally, but also metaphorically. In *In Our Time*, Nick Adams has moved away from the safety and security of a sheltered life at home to the theatre of a war-torn Europe. In *The Sun Also Rises*, Jake Barnes is an American who keeps on moving about in Paris and Spain. In *A Farewell to Arms*, Frederic Henry joins the Italian army and fights for a cause he does not really or adequately understand. And in *For Whom the Bell Tolls*, Robert Jordan, though a sincere and dedicated individual is not very sure of his political affiliations because he finds that the Fascists are not all black and that the Loyalists are not all white. They do not believe in rhetoric; in fact, they are usually reticent, and take recourse to understatements, to clipped sentences. The Hemingway heroes have little to do with conventional morality, and Hemingway himself is utterly forthright on this point. These heroes, no doubt, are defeated victims, injured both within and without, but, while experiencing their defeat, they weave an invisible armour or shield of their code around themselves so that for the most part they remain undefeated.

While the Hemingway heroes are young and inexperienced people, lost and confused in this world bereft of values, but still trying to grope their ways with the help of a tenuously workable code, the code heroes, 'the tutor', are usually older men who have become what they had to become. In a way, they have realized their potentialities and discovered the areas of their operation, and that is why the moment they step out of their chosen areas, they are on slippery ground. In Hemingway's short story, "In Another Country", the Major cries over the death of his wife, even though he has encountered and dealt with death all his life. In *The Sun Also Rises*, Romero, the bull-fighter, refuses to accept defeat at the hands of Robert Cohn who has been the boxing champion at Princeton. In the bull ring too he faces the bulls squarely without letting his physical injuries impede his performance. In *The Old Man and the Sea*, Santiago does not let the Merlin escape in spite of his old age, hunger, exhaustion and the fear that he might lose. He fights out the battle to its bitter end until he is successful. It is with the same or similar kind of courage and perseverance that he defends his prize against the sharks; he does not give in, and he does attain a superhuman stature because of his epic struggle against utterly heavy and nearly insurmountable odds.

It cannot be said that these code heroes are more successful than the Hemingway heroes; the truth lies in the fact that even as they suffer physical defeat, they win an extraordinary kind of moral victory. Santiago loses the Merlin, the giant fish, its flesh having been eaten up by the sharks; however, he does have the immense satisfaction of doing all that he could do in the given situation. And it is this satisfaction, this feeling of incredible, yet real involvement that lends him dignity and grandeur.

As we make this distinction between the 'tyro' and the 'tutor', between the Hemingway hero and the code hero, of necessity we have to reckon with fact that in spite of all their oddities and perversions the Hemingway heroes too, like their code counterparts, have their own code of conduct that guides them through the travails and traumas of life.

Jack Barnes is the narrator-hero of *The Sun Also Rises*; he is reportedly a journalist and an expatriate; he is an American who has been living in France after the First World War Jack has been wounded in the war; he has been hit in the genitals, and as result of this injury he has been emasculated. Jack's emotional, psychological injuries are far deeper than his physical wounds; he is, at any rate, a seemingly dissolute person. He cannot enjoy sex, and quite naturally his relation with Brett Ashley loses much of their meaning and significance. Jack's emotional, psychological injuries are far deeper than his physical wounds. Jack does not seen to have any stable identity of his own, for, as we find him, he exists only in relation with the other characters in the novel. However, there is a positive side to his character that he is very close to nature. It is, therefore, not at all strange that in spite of all his handicaps and shortcomings Jake has come to terms with life and has evolved a code in order to be able to endure it. "I try and play it along and just not make trouble for people" is the motto of Jack's life, and despite all disenchantments with life he hopes to sail through the currents of life with the help of this very code.

Another important figure in this novel is Pedro Romero who is a great bullfighter. He has been trained at a bullfighting school. Basically, he is a man of polite manners, and is respectful to others. It is indeed by a peculiar quirk of fate that, through Jack Barnes, he gets in touch with Brett Ashley. Romero's purity and innocence and simplicity disarm Brett; she realizes that she has been spoiling him, and she leaves him almost in huff. But by the time she does so, he has brought about in her a vital change in her outlook and behavior. Romero is a man of great virility and physical strength. He dominates the scene in nearly one-third of the novel, and it is in view of his perseverance and firmness of will that Philip Young calls him Hemingway's 'early code hero' (O'Connor, W.V. 1964).

Count Mippipopolous, no doubt, is one of the secondary characters in *The Sun Also Rises,* and yet he is fully individualized and well-delineated character. He has been a participant in several wars and four revolutions, and has sustained injuries in them. He has a special fondness for antiquities, solitude and brandy, and though he believes, generally speaking, in the efficacy of love, Brett Ashley dismisses him as someone "dead" (Hemingway 1974). He is guided by his own code. His code is never to joke, for joking makes enemies. He may not be a code character in the accepted sense of the term, and still he is a code character, for he does follow a self-evolved code of values for his moral and spiritual sustenance.

A Farewell to Arms is a novel that takes us to a world ravaged by war, by cholera and syphilis, by "frostbites, chilblains, jaundice, gonorrhea, self-inflicted wounds, pneumonia and hard and soft chancres" (Hemingway, 1975); it is a world dominated by sickness and gloom and depression and disillusionment, yet it is a world enlivened and redeemed by happiness and joy and bliss, by love and compassion. Frederick Henry, the protagonist, comes to Europe, to Italy, as a student of architecture at Rome. He is not a tourist; he is only a displaced and uprooted person, and it is for unexplained, unidentified reason, perhaps for the sake of adventure alone, that he joins the Italian war as an ambulance driver. Initially Frederick Henry strikes us as a flippant character, a cynical person. Curiously enough, and perhaps foolhardily enough, Frederick thinks that he is immortal and that nothing would happen to him in the war. However, Frederick gets grievously wounded in the war, and during the long period of treatment he undergoes at the hospital, he moves closer and closer still to Catherine Barkley. His idea of war as a glorious phenomenon and of the battlefield as a place for making noble sacrifices is rudely shattered. Hereafter we encounter a completely changed Frederick, a person of strong will and great determination, one who has gathered a good deal directly from life and whose actions are based on conviction. The mere fact that he jumps into the flooded, swollen Taglimanto for his escape from the army at a grave threat to his life signifies the centrality of his newly-evolved code, his commitment to peace and love in life. And his unbroken, unflinching love for Catherine Barkley for the sake of peace and bliss in life is a positive achievement in itself. However, the truth of the matter is that Frederick Henry is a character who may, with certain reservations or qualifications, be looked upon as a code character, for, in spite of his initial flippancy, vagrancy and cynicism, he conducts himself, later in his life, according to his own code of values which he evolves out of his desperate and ugly struggles with life.

To Have and Have Not is not quite an important novel, and yet it deserves consideration chiefly because its hero, Harry Morgan, is a code character and that the way in which he conducts himself has his own bearing on Hemingway's concept of the code hero. The present novel consists of three interlinked stories. In Part one of the novel entitled "Henry Morgan: Spring", Morgan becomes extremely poor because one of the rich business magnates cheats him of his legitimate dues. As such, he is compelled to adopt questionable means to earn his livelihood, and in the process loses his arm and his boat. In Part Two Hemingway describes Harry Morgan's extremely happy domestic life in utter contrast to the unhappy domestic life of the other characters in the novel. In the final part, Part Three, of the novel entitled "Harry Morgan: Winter", Harry undertakes to carry a few Cubans out of the United States. The Cubans get into a boat that he has hired, but on their way to Cuba, as Harry tries to kill the Cubans, he himself is fatally wounded.

The main burden of the present novel is the severity of the economic depression that hit America during the thirties, and though this book does also deal with the theme of domesticity, of close-knit family relationship, basically it brings out Hemingway's awareness of the contrast between the rich and the poor, the have and the have-nots. Harry Morgan is the first protagonist in Hemingway's novels to have been individualized through his physical features. He is a man of solid physical build; he has his own determination, single-mindedness, self-command and capacity for endurance. He begins his life as a man of action; initially he is rank individualist, and it is no surprise that he choose to become a pirate. However, at the end of his life he realizes that a man cannot do or achieve anything all by himself and that he must accept society and work in harmony with it. Harry Morgan is a code hero who impresses us as the very image of virility and self-confidence, as one who evolves his code out of his own eventful life and transmits it to the world in the hope of doing well to humanity.

For Whom the Bell Tolls is not a flawless novel, first, because it deals with a rather idealized and romantic love story; secondly, because the story in it appears to be one of melodramatic struggle rather than of conviction, and, lastly, because the protagonist of the novel, Robert Jordan, does not seem to be experienced enough to say what he does actually speak to the other characters in the book. And still, through a treatment of Jordan's life and death, through the very manner of his dying, Hemingway is able to impress upon us the basic idea that in spite of all odds life has its own attractions, that life is really worth living, and that there are causes worth dying for. In the present novel Hemingway describes three days, nearly seventy hours, in the life of Robert Jordan. He is fighting as an American volunteer in the Spanish Civil War, and is sent to a guerrilla camp in the mountains near Segovia to destroy an important bridge there in order to stall the advance of the enemy forces. Jordan spends three days and three nights in the cave of the guerrillas, waiting there for the assault on the bridge to materialize, and in the meantime falls in love with Maria whose father, a Republican mayor, has been murdered by the Falangists and who herself has been raped by them. Jordan is not very sure if he would be able to destroy the bridge; he is not at all sure of the timing of the assault too; nevertheless, he moves forward and blows up the bridge, but in the process gets grievously wounded and is left to die all by himself. We may lament the manner in which Jordan has been abandoned to die, and we may look upon his death as something cruel and humiliating, and yet the novel has offered us its prize that no sacrifice, perhaps, is too big to make human life better and more worth living.

Robert Jordan is a character who has plenty of courage, strength and valor, and who may and does risk everything, his life itself, for the achievement of his goal. He is not a conscript, and he does not stumble into war or embrace it in the spirit of adventure. Jordan is one of those protagonists that Hemingway has tried to present to us in bold and vivid physical terms. He is young, tall and thin. Later, Jordan becomes a teacher of Spanish at Montana from where he joins the civil war in Spain. He is an intellectual; he has been a teacher and also a writer, but the moment he realizes that his mind is likely to interfere with his zeal for action, he decides to stop making an exercise of it. Jordan is in full command of himself; he has nothing to do with sham heroism, and he certainly harbors no illusions. He knows his intentions; he knows as well the true nature of the Spanish people and the officers participating in the war, and but for the cause to which he has pledged himself, he would have gone in for a life with Maria in place of dangers and death. His personality has its own magnetism, and it is for very understandable reasons that Anselmo and Pilar and El Sordo, and even Pablo, get drawn towards him and respect him. Robert Jordan is full of his sense of duty; in his devotion to work he ignores the pleasures of life, and he believes in the Republic "with fervor as those who have religious faith believe in the mysteries" (Hemingway 89). The motive that inspires him to participate in the Spanish Civil War is clear; like the 'partzans', he is fighting so that eventually; there should be no more danger and so that the country should be a good place to live in! (Hemingway 158).

Robert Jordan may be a Hemingway hero, as he indeed is, and still he is a code hero, for his character has undergone great changes, and he has built strong defenses around himself. He is a man of action, of determined action, and, as we have seen, all that he does is inspired by his commitment to a code of values.

Although, as Philip Young puts it, *Across into the Trees* "reads like a parody of Hemingway's earlier works" (P. Young 1964), and although in this novel "the distance that Hemingway once maintained between himself and his protagonist has disappeared" (P. Young 1964), still we have reasons to believe that because of the presence of certain qualities in him, the protagonist of this novel does deserve to be called a code hero.

The protagonist in this novel, Richard Cantwell, has been a professional soldier; he is now fifty-one, and has, not unnaturally, acquired a good deal of experience and worldly wisdom. He has fought gallantly in World Wars I and II, and has received both physical and emotional wounds. He has his right hand, head and his body in general injured in the war; his heart has become weak, and his face has been disfigured. He has lost the love of the three women who were there earlier in his life, and he is now in love with Renata, a Venus-like girl of nineteen. At the same time he is also obsessed with the sin of issuing foolish orders to his men during the war, resulting in terrible loss of human lives. At his age Cantwell is shorn of most of his illusions and romantic ideas, and it is quite in a characteristic vein that he says: "Everything is much smaller when you are older" (Hemingway 1966). Commenting on the character of the Grand Master, Hemingway says: "He was truly handsome as a man should be, from the inside out, so that his smile starts from his heart, or whatever is the center of the body, and comes frankly beautifully to the surface, which is the face" (Hemingway 1966). And this is exactly how the novelist paints Cantwell's character. Cantwell moves about with superb confidence and with a well-defined plan of being kind, decent and good to people. Precisely speaking, it is this very disillusioned, but sturdy, aspect of Cantwell's character that gives us the first distinct ideas of his being a code hero.

Cantwell, being aged and mature, is not at all interested in the ordinary pleasures of life; instead, he is in search of perfection, of something stable and enduring, so that he may find himself in a position to make the most of his life. It is indeed something remarkable to see that Cantwell is not afraid of death and that he faces death or the idea of death with boldness and courage. He is a man of tremendous will-power, and whenever he tends to feel depressed, he cheers himself up by saying: "Cheer up, boy.... So don't be gloomy, boy, or man" (Hemingway 1966). The truth is that he offers a challenge to death when he declares: "... you can sheathe your seythe, old brother death, if you have got a sheath for it. Or...you can take your seythe and stick it" (Hemingway 1966). Cantwell addresses death as his "old brother" because throughout his life he has been dangerously close to it. He may, with due reservations, be accepted as a code hero, not really because of his revulsion against war or because of his passion for the life of the senses, but because of his superb self-confidence, his commitment to the principle of honor and his bold defiance of death. Like Robert Jordon, Cantwell too is a citizen of the world, for though he is an American, he belongs as well to Italy and Venice where he has shed his blood; and he reminds us also of Santiago because of his defiance of death and his fierce commitment to his conviction.

Robert Jordon and Cantwell are code characters in a rather special sense, but Santiago's case is different. He is distinct and distinctive kind of code hero, and as such his character demands treatment on a much wider and deeper scale.

The Old Man and the Sea is perhaps a long short story or a very short novel rather than a novel proper; it is "an epic metaphor for life, a contest in which even the problem of right and wrong seems paltry before the great thing that is the struggle" (Young 1964), and it may as well be read "as an allegory entirely personal to its author, as an account of his own struggle, his determination, and his literary vicissitudes" (Young 1964). In any case, the protagonist of this book, Santiago, is outstandingly a code hero, whose message to mankind is that "while a man may grow old, and be wholly down on his luck, he can still dare, stick to the rules, persist when he is licked, and thus by the manner of his losing victory" (Young 1964).

Santiago is an old Cuban fisherman. After eighty-four days without a fish, he ventures far out to sea alone, and hooks a giant marlin in the Gulf Stream. For two days and two nights the old man holds on while he is towed farther out to sea; finally, he brings the fish alongside, harpoons it, to take his prize away from him. He kills them all until he has only his broken tiller to fight with. By that time, however, the sharks have eaten up everything except the skeleton which the old fisherman tows to the shore. Half-dead with exhaustion, he makes his ways to bed to sleep and dream of other days and things.

Santiago is "a strange old man" (Hemingway 1967); in fact, "everything about him was old except his eyes" (Hemingway, 1967). Although, for obvious reasons, he is considered to be "definitely and finally *salao,* which is the worst form of unlucky" (Hemingway 1967), "he looks at things, in spite of his moments of depression, with his; sun-burned, confident loving eyes" (Hemingway 1966). Santiago is indeed a picture of self-confidence, but at the same time he is also an image of humility. "He was" says Hemingway, "too simple to wonder when he had attained humility. But he knew he had attained it and he knew it was not disgraceful and it carried no loss of true pride" (Hemingway 1967). Santiago is not a religious man, and yet the pictures in color of the Sacred Heart of Jesus and the virgin of cobre keep hanging on the walls of his shack. It is very frequently that he dreams of the days of his boyhood and youth, of Africa, and of lions on the beaches in the evening. It is with an obvious sense of exhilaration that he speaks to Manolin about his great strength and vigor in his youth, but he loses no time in telling the boy: "I may not be as strong as I think.... But I know tricks and I have resolution" (Hemingway 1967).

After a dry and unlucky spell of eighty-four days, it is on the eighty-fifth day that Santiago goes out on the sea for fishing with a sense of trepidation as also of determination. Over the years Santiago has identified himself with the sea, with the wind that blows over it, with the sky that covers it, and with the creatures that live in it; truly speaking, there is something elemental about him. "He had", observes Hemingway, "no mysticism about turtles although he had gone in turtle beats for many years.... Most people are heartless about turtles because a turtle's heart will beat for hours after he has been cut up and butchered. But the old man thought, I have such a heart too and my feet and hands are like theirs" (Hemingway 1967). Besides other things, Santiago is also a picture of love and affection and tender feelings.

Armed with his stamina and stubbornness, everyday is 'a new day' (Hemingway 1967). He thinks it is better to be lucky (Hemingway 1967). On the eighty-fifth day he is lucky enough to hook a giant marlin, but he finds it terribly difficult to control it or to pull it into his boat. And it is from this very moment that his epic fight with the fish begins. For two days and two nights he stays out on the sea, struggling, despairing, trying again and again, thinking, and talking to himself or to the fish. "Fish" he says, "I love you and respect you very much. But I will kill you dead" (Hemingway, 1967). In a highly poetic and poignant manner, Hemingway describes his predicament, his feeling of being all alone far out on the sea in a trying and tense situation: "The old man had seen many great fish. He had seen many that weighed more than a thousand pounds and he had caught two of that size in his life, but never alone. The author puts it, his "determination to kill him never relaxed in his sorrow for him" (Hemingway 1967). In fact, his mind works on two interlinked levels: "I must kill him and keep strong to do it" (Hemingway 1967). Santiago is haunted by his sense of loneliness too:

> ...he began to pity the great fish that he had hooked.
>
> He is wonderful and strange and who knows how old he is, he thought.
>
> Never have I had such a strong fish nor one who acted so strangely.
>
> Perhaps he is too wise to jump....
>
> I wonder if he has any plans or if he is just as desperate as I am? (Hemingway 1967)

The novelist goes further, and this is how he brings out the fisherman's tortured psychology: "His choices had been to stay in the deep dark water far out beyond all snares and traps and treacheries. My choice was to go there to find him beyond all people. Santiago is at his wit's end. His patience, his perseverance, his doggedness is there, and he has decided that he would give up neither the fight nor the fish, and yet old fisherman feels miserable and helpless. He goes on trying and trying. Santiago has won the battle, and what has sustained him all through is his stamina, his vigor. The old man is perhaps too much tired and broken to realize that he is in for yet another spell of serious encounter. He is now without any weapon; the sharks eat up the entire flesh of the fish, and what the old fisherman brings to the coast is just the huge skeleton of the giant fish.

Santiago is a man of stupendous courage, and his old age is certainly no handicap to him. He is a code character, not merely because he is man of bold and brave action, but because he goes by his code of values according to which he just refuses to accept defeat.... "Man is not made for defeat", says he, "A man can be destroyed but not defeated" (Hemingway 1967). Success or failure is not at all important and significant in his scale of values; what is really important and significant there is man's commitment to action, his determination to carry on his struggle against all odds and obstructions, his stubbornness to defy defeat. The old fisherman, all alone far out on the sea and nearly defenseless, fights with the great marlin and the dangerous sharks, with elemental forces, for two days and two nights, and in the process gets bruised, injured, and terribly fatigued. And even though he carries to the coast just the skeleton of the huge fish, in his heart he carries the satisfaction and the pride of having fought to the last ounce of his energy and strength. Santiago is an exemplary character, an epic character, a heroic character, indeed a code character. The symbolical dimensions of Santiago's character may invoke different and differing interpretations, but there is, or could be, absolutely no confusion about his identity as a code character.

It is indeed true that Hemingway's heroes are expatriate and rootless people, but it is also true that, in their own ways, they are honest, virile and sensitive people. They have seen the nothingness and despair and death at the centre of the world; they are terribly aware of the milieu or situation they find themselves placed in. Through his heroes Hemingway has shown what right conduct is or could be in a given situation, and these situations usually are of an extreme nature dealing with varied crises in human life.

Works Cited

Fenton, A. Charles. *The Apprenticeship of Ernest Hemingway* (New York, 1954), 13.

Hemingway, E. *Across the River and into the Trees* (New York, 1966), 13.

——. *A Farewell to Arms* (Penguin ed., 1975), 13.

——. *For Whom the Bell Tolls* (Penguin ed., 1964), 89.

——. *The Old Man and The Sea* (Moscow, 1967), 43.

——. *The Sun Also Rises* (Penguin ed., 1974), 51.

Lania, L. *Hemingway* (New York, 1961), 5.

O'Connor, W.V. (ed.). *Seven Modern American Novelists: An Introduction* (New York, 1964), 152.

Rovit, Earl. *Ernest Hemingway* (New York, 1963), 85.

Wegenknecht, Edward. *Cavalcade of the American Novel* (Calcutta, 1969), 373.

Young, P. *Modern American Novelists: An Introduction* (New York, 1964), 158.

□

Dividing Concerns in Khushwant Singh's Novel *Train to Pakistan*

Mukunda Upadhyaya

Khushwant Singh was born in 1915 in a village called Sargoda, which is now in Pakistan and died on 20 March 2014 at his Delhi-based residence at the age of 99. He studied in Delhi and Lahore and moved to King's College, London. Practiced at Lahore Court before joining the Indian Ministry of External Affairs in 1947. With 64 books to his credit, Khushwant Singh done well the triple role, as a short-story writer, novelist and religious historian. As a religious historian his most enduring work has been in the field of Sikh history and an autobiography *Truth, Love and Little Malice* his brilliant portrait of Ranjit Singh vividly brings out the leader, the ruler and the Man. Khushwant Singh's long spell as a journalist and his trips to abroad in his professional capacity had brought him into contact with different kinds of people and varieties of experience. He was a product of Western education and culture but he claims "I am, if I may coin the word, an Orio-Occident". These influences can be traced in his works. He was the one novelist who successfully and realistically presented the events in his novels. He established himself as a distinguished writer of social realism with the publication of his first novel *Train to Pakistan* in 1956. This novel won him international acclaim along with Grove India Fiction Prize. The novel has a grim story of individuals and communities caught in the whirlpool of division of the Indian subcontinent into two states—India and Pakistan in 1947. As M.K. Naik rightly observes,

> The impact of partition (division) on a small village on the Indo-Pakistan border is shown here with pitiless realism of description and the swift tempo of the narrative carries the reader along.

Train to Pakistan projects with precision a picture of the fearful horrors enacted on the Indo-Pakistan border during the fear haunted days of August 1947. The leaders of the country were solely responsible for these horrors as they sow the seeds of communal suspicion. The novel describes in vivid terms, the grossness, ghastliness and total insanity of the two-nation theory and the division tragedy. It also conveys obviously the pity and horror of division.

The novel is the touching tale of a village, Mano Majra, struck down by the hate and violence that came with the division of the subcontinent when a train-load of massacred men, women and children arrive in the village. The predominant features of the novel are its stark realism, its absolute fidelity to the truth and above all, its trenchant exposure of the division-horrors. Mano Majra, a remote village in the north-western region of undivided India, serves as the fictional setting of the novel. Although traditionally devoid of political consciousness, the village emerges as a microcosm of India. As Hindus and Sikhs battled their Muslim 'brothers' for a political stronghold in the newly liberated nation India, the villagers' traditional ways of life progressively disintegrated into selfishness, mistrust and cruelty. Lala Ram Lal, a Hindu moneylender, was murdered by a dacoit, Malli, but the police bungled the case in such a way that the Sikhs of the village began to look askance at the Muslims. The villagers were carried away when they saw people from either side of the boundary on their way, seeking refuse and security. Most of the Sikhs were all rage when they had come to know that their Sikh brethern had been subjected to heinous cruelties by the Muslims in Pakistan. The Muslims in the village were dazed at the predatory advances of the Sikhs in the surrounding villages and resolved to leave for Pakistan, the land of Islamic faith and promise. But the Sikhs were unrelented and would not like to leave the Muslims unscathed. They stretched a wine rope across the bridge in order to kill the people sitting on the roof of the train. However, Jugga, a Sikh, slashed at the rope whereby he sets an example of supreme sacrifice. He puts an end to his life for the sake of enabling the Muslims, particularly his beloved, Nooran, to reach Pakistan safely. The love story is used to the exigencies of the political upheaval (division), which along with the conflicting motives of the leaders at the helm of affairs, are not dealt with comprehensively as Nahal does in *Azadi*.

How harmony degenerates into disharmony is traced with humanistic concern. Khushwant Singh projects Mano Majrans as bright and breezy, contented a calm during the tumultuous times while most of the other villages in the country were reeling under the burden of Communalism. In their happy ignorance of ghastly riots the Muslims and Sikhs of this village still clung to ideas preached by Gandhi, even though Gandhi himself was then "walking the bloody paths of the riot-torn India of his dream, lonely and disillusioned. "Nevertheless, Mano Majra seems to be typical where people belonging to various religions lived in amity. To quote K.R. Srinivasa Iyengar "Here's functional 'integration'", and indeed there are tens of thousands of villages like Mano Majra, where the law has always been peaceful Co-existence, and not Communal strife." With the arrival of the ghost-train the age-old harmony between the communities was shattered but the Sikhs of the village did not nourish any ill-will, though communal passions had been in the air because of division of the country.

Khushwant Singh shows when things go pell-mell, even the majority will be afflicted with fear complex which is further accentuated by a faulty reading of history. When things are misrepresented the consequences are ghastly and reason and logic are put behind. It started with the murder of Lala Ram Lal by a Malli, a dacoit. The murder was interpreted in such a way that in no time it gained communal overtones. The police enquiry had sown the seeds of mistrust among the Muslims and the Hindus. The doubt of the police about the Mano Majrans and the whereabouts of Sultana and Iqbal made the Sikhs look at Muslim Community with an air of suspicion. In fact, the visit of the police "had divided Mano Majra into two halves as neatly as a Knife cuts through a pat of butter" (105). The whole Sikh Community sank into silence and was anxious to distinguish friends from foes. The recollection of the faint smell of searing flesh which they had been burnt a few days ago, sent 'a chill down their spine'. Similarly, Iqbal's reported aim to spy on them was another shock and this jolted them out of the Cocoon of complacency and well-being. The seeds of suspicion spread rapidly as both the communities adopted diametrically opposite and hostile position with their faulty understanding of history for the British were mainly responsible. The British historian stressed the point that the Muslims and others had urged wars only on religious grounds. The Britishers, thus, encouraged as many divisions as they could resulted in Communal carnage. Iyenger says "There is enough evidence to convict the British administrators who after a hundred years of trusteeship could only prepare for the holocaust." The leader of the group asked the people to take revenge constantly harping on the words 'Hindu', 'Sikh', and 'Muslim' in order to work them into furies. In an interview to Amitava Kumar, Khushwant Singh has observed, "When we got Independence we were all under the illusion that the communal divide is now over once and for all. It was British who encouraged it. They were gone and there would be no more communal tension in the country. That proved to be wrong. We have had more communal violence since Independence. Hindu-Muslim riots and even Hindu-Sikh riots and Hindu-Christian violence gone to an almost nauseating extent.

> ...for each Hindu or Sikh they kill, kill two Mussulmans. For each Woman they abduct or rape, abduct two... (129). Religion thus with 'soulless world' could only be the cause of barriers creating disharmony amongst different sects.

Division is, it has been argued, the result of the failure of 'Gandhi Caps', those leaders preaching non-violence. But Khushwant Singh seems uninterested to delve deep into the motives of the leaders, who were, in one way or the other way round, accountable for the division and the mass hysteria that followed it. Nevertheless, the writer appears to give vent to his feeling in the case of Jawaharlal Nehru, who failed to act and to rise to the occasion.

> ...Where was the power?.... Long ago we made a tryst with destiny and now the time comes when we shall redeem our pledge not wholly or in the fully measure but very substantially. Yes, Mr. Prime Minister, you made your tryst. So did many others on the 15th August, Independence Day. (122)

Perhaps it is not correct to blame Nehru squarely for what happened during the days of division. It may be plausible to argue that "the prince of Hamlet; Nehru, could not rise to the occasion. He was said to be "physically ill at the stark, direct confrontation with the miseries overwhelming so many of his countrymen". Like other leaders, he too was stunned by the magnitude of the carnage and the communal cruelty of which his people had suddenly shown themselves capable was a shocking revelation to him. He was said to be "physically ill at the stark, direct confrontation with the miseries overwhelming so many of his countrymen".

Khushwant Singh is very critical when he unfolds Iqbal, a replica of a cunning political leader in the grab of Socialism who came to Mano Majra not to stem in communal carnage and make sacrifice but to watch the drama at the village as it was 'a vital point for refugee movement'.

His mission was to keep the village unaffected by communalism. Towards the conclusion, he came to know that no corner was free from "the contagion of communal virus". When he was told that the train heading to Pakistan with Muslim refugees from Mano Majra would be attacked, in a fit of emotion, the thought of sacrifying himself in an attempt to avert the tragedy. But he found sacrifice futile if there was none to see and admire the supreme act. The rough Jugga—"a self-confessed *budmash*—after his release, came to know the attack on the train must mean danger to his Nooran, a Muslim girl. He made up his mind to prevent the attack, if necessary at the risk of his own life. According to the plan of the avengers, a rope "stiff as a shaft of steel" was tied across the first Span of the bridge to finish off the passengers boarded on the train. With his *kirpan*, he slashed at the rope that was designed to bring about the train disaster. "There is a volley of shots. The man shivers and collapses". The rope snapped in the centre as he fell. "The train went over him, and went on to Pakistan" with all Muslim refugees. Whatever be the motivation for his action, the fact remains that he did the incredible. It may be, as Srinivasa Iyenger puts it "a speck in the dust-whirl that was the partition (division)." The passion of one man saved hundreds of innocent people. To quote Chirantan Kulshrestha:

> Jugga's act of love and his sacrifice silhouetted against the backdrop of hatred and violence, towers above the communal differences and lends a meaning to the general aimlessness of life in the partition (division) days. Thus Jugga's sacrifice has shown that the heart of the lovers is un-divided though the nation has divided leading to communal hatred and disharmony. His sacrifice is motivated by personal love expanding itself into the love of an entire community. He saves the whole train load of innocent Muslims at the cost of his own life and follows the basic tenets of Sikhism which preaches undiscriminating love for all.

Imam Bakhs a *mullah* of the mosque had a sorrowful and miserable experiences of life. "His wife and only son had died within a few days of each other" (79). He lost eye-sight and became a beggar with his baby girl Nooran. Events move fast in the novel and Imam Baksh was compelled to leave Mano Majra against his will. He had to go to Pakistan for safety as with other Muslims of that area. He says to Meet Singh thus:

> What have we to do with Pakistan. We were born here. So were our ancestors. We have lived amongst you as brothers. (126)

The above passage shows Bakh's unwillingness to leave India, even though the country has split into two nations—Hindu India and Muslim Pakistan.

One important character in the novel is Mr. Hukum Chand, the Magistrate and Deputy Commissioner of the district. He comes to Mano Majra rest-house and enquires the law and order situation. The Inspector reports him that peace prevails there. The Magistrate cautions the Inspector to keep an eye on Mano Majra as it is the most important village on the border to Pakistan. Thus, the country has divided and Indian Administration is keen on keeping law and order intact in the country after division.

Train to Pakistan presents the Indian perception of the traumatic experience which is free from religious bias. Khushwant Singh himself states: "I think it is a documentary novel of the partition (division), an extremely tragic event which hurt me very much. I had no animosity against either the Muslims or Pakistanis, but I felt that I should do something to express that point of view" (12). Though he was not the sufferer of the riots, he knows the miseries that division had unleashed.

Since the novel deals with the theme of division which is very expansive, the writer should be on guard in evolving a suitable technique lest his realism degenerates into mere 'historical documentary'. So the technique he adopts should be such as to capture the spectrum of the cataclysmic events. Khushwant Singh's realistic portrayal seems to be successful since his art is revealed not merely in the profound probing into the real, but also in the transformation of the actual into symbols and images. The long rainless summer symbolizes heavenly retribution for the communal riots. The weather, scorching sun and swelling rivers stand for the violence escalating beyond comprehension. The train is also a powerful symbol. Mano Majra was guided by the trains and it was when the ghost train passed through the village that the quiet and harmonious life came to a halt. Also there is a pungent irony in the novel. The Sikh militant planning to wreak vengeance on the Muslims chanted the verse from the Scriptures.

> By the grace of God
> We bear the world nothing but goodwill. (132)

However, Jugga's sacrifice got religious sanction. Singh has succeeded, through resolved limitation and rigorous selection, in communicating to his readers a hint of the grossness, ghastliness of the division tragedy.

As the very first novelist on division, Khushwant Singh is successful in that he portrays the harsh facts of life against the background of India's division, its skillful dissection of the real. The compelling story of people in turmoil is far broader in its implications than its length might suggest. The novelist seems to deprecate the part played by the educated people of the country in causing devastation, making an irony of the whole movement of freedom. However, he does not offer penetrating insights into the causes of division and the reasons for the sudden blindness with which the leaders were afflicted during those fateful days. Nevertheless, the novel appears unparalleled in its objective and realistic treatment of division.

Works Cited

Anjaneyulu, T. *A Critical Study of the Selected Novels of Mulk Raj Anand, Manohar Malgonkar and Khushwant Singh.* New Delhi: Atlantic Publishers and Distributors, 1998.

Kulshresth. "Khushwant Singh's Fiction," Consideration. Ed. Minakshi Mukharjee (Bombay: Allied Publishers), 126.

Rao, V. Pala Prasad, Rani N. Nirupa, Rao D.B. Haskara. *India-Pakistan, Partition Perspectives in Indo-English Novels.* New Delhi: Discovery Publishing House, 2004.

Shahane, V.A. *Khushwant Singh* (New York: Twayne Publishers 1972), 79.

Singh, Khushwant. *Train to Pakistan.* New Delhi: The Books International, 1989.

□

The Aurobindonian and the Post-Aurobindonian Traditions in Indian English Poetry: A Contrastive Study of the Representative Poets

Radhakant Mishra

Tradition in art, literature and culture inevitably undergoes with the passage of time a vicissitude in any nation of the world. This law of change also occurs in the evolution of a new tradition in literature. From this angle of vision, if we retrospectively review the past trend of Indian English poetry, we notice progressive transmutation of its features from poet to poet from the time of Derozio up to post-modern period.

In this context of metamorphosis of tradition of Indian English poetry, attempt is sought to demarcate two traditions exploiting the traits of Aurobindonian poetry as the basis of distinction.

This article expatiates comprehensively upon the distinctive features of the Aurobindonian and the post-Aurobindonian poetry in English with a view to highlighting the dissimilarities existing in the traditions of Indian English poetry. It focuses on the bifurcation of avenue of poetry in terms of trend and tradition and establishes two distinctive traditions that are analysed in the article on the basis of constrastive study of the poets of the pre- and post-periods.

At the advent of new modernism in post-India an ideological cleavage occurred in the community of Indian Poets writing in English and resulted in their classification into the Aurobindonians and the post-Aurobindonians. This classification, which was made by P. Lal the founder of the Writers Workshop and his co-worker K. Raghavendra Rao on the basis of the new poets' response and reaction to the poetry of Sri Aurobindo led to a kind of rivalry and hostility between two groups of poets. Each group of poets asserted in poetry an identity and individuality of its own. They differed radically from each other in their conception of the mode and technique of versification.

The stream of Aurobindonian poetry that emerged from the poetical works of the pre-Aurobindonians like H.L.V. Derozio, Kashi Prasad Ghose, Michael Madhusudan, Toru Dutt and Manmohan Ghose gradually widened it breadth by assuming exuberantly romantic and mystical character. This trend of Aurobindonian poetry perpetuated till the dawn of post-modernism in the wake of which it declined due to predominant influence of new ideological theories and concepts. The evolution of new theories such as post-modernism, Marxism, feminism and existentialism, paved the path for emergence of post-Aurobindonian poetry known as new poetry. The new poets were inspired by the Writers Workshop to write poetry in accordance with the canons of Kavita Manifesto introduced by the poets P. Lal and Raghavendra Rao. The new poets of the post-Aurobindonian tradition intellectually opposed the Aurobindonian tradition of poetry evolved by Sri Aurobindo and sustained by his adherents. With this objective in view they characterized their verses with new ingredients such as new themes of sociological interest, surrealism, private voice, colloquialism, new idioms and jargons. They exploited all these traits as advocated by the Writers Workshop founded in 1959.

The new poets who invariably denounced the past poetic convention adhered to by the Aurobindonians, often reviewed retrospectively their poetical works to derive inspiration from their versification. They, however, revolutionized their own trend of writing and reshaped their mode and artifice of versification in an altogether new mould but without ignoring the traditional value sustained by their predecessors. M.K. Naik contends "the modernist poets who are militant modernists stand on the shoulders of the older poets".[1]

The post-Aurobindonian poetry blossomed out after the appearance of Nissim Ezekiel as a harbinger of new poets in the new horizon of Indian poetry in English. He is pre-eminently a major voice that represents the change of an era in the domain of Indian English poetry. Ezekiel is an outstanding poet in terms of his wealth of literary output and sustained quality of verse. He is the first post-poet who inaugurated a new tradition of poetry, which was later on invigorated by his successors P. Lal, R. Rao, Pritish Nandy, Parthasarathy, Daruwalla, Adil Jussawalla and above all by Kamala Das, Gauri Deshpande, Mamta Kalia and other women poets. All these new post-Aurobindonian poets waged a war against Sri Aurobindo and his adherents with the weapon of new modernist poetry that undermined their poetic tradition and overshadowed their achievements as poets. The overwhelming sentiments of modernism and the influence of this new theory gradually weaned poets away from the Aurobindonian tradition of versification.

The emergence of Sri Aurobindo as a poet ushered a new tradition in to Indian poetry in English. His exquisite thematic exploitation of myths and legends, innovation of new mode, diction and artifice of versification infatuated many of his contemporary poets, who formed a school of poets and became the practitioners of the poetic convention known as Aurobindonian tradition of poetry. Sri Aurobindo and his adherents initiated a new tradition that flourished luxuriantly till its culmination in the publication of his epic Savitri in 1950.

Let us first analyse the characteristics of the poetry of the Aurobindonian tradition in order to differentiate it from that of the post-Aurobindonian modernist poets. The distinctly marked features of their poetry are pointed out contrastively in the following paragraphs.

The Aurobindonians were the practitioners of religious, mystical, philosophical and meditative verses. The poetical works of Sri Aurobindo, N.K. Gupta, D.K. Roy, K.D. Sethna, Nirodbaran, Anilbaran, Romen and Prithwindra give ample evidence of this kind of poetry. They keenly responded to the values of legends, myths and mystical ideas. The post-Aurobindonians on the other hand reacted against this kind of poetry of imagination and vision. Instead of savouring the myths and legends and the Vedantic and mystical ideas drawn from the past of India, they responded to the psychological, social, economic and cultural issues of the contemporary society. The post-Aurobindonians committed to writing verses with an anti-Aurobindonian interest outlook and spirit imbibing the mode style and technique innovated by Ezekiel, Dom Moraes, Kamala Das, P. Lal, R. Rao, Daruwalla and Shiv K. Kumar. It is axiomatic that the post-Aurobindonians were basically anti-Aurobindonians, who pioneered a new tradition of versification in response to the new modernist concepts and conventionalized the new mode of writing for the new poets of the post-era. With an unflinching commitment they embarked upon the new tradition of writing verses in an unprecedented new fashion with a view to imparting a new identity and dimension to new poetry. Their verses bear the stamp of their anti-Aurobindonian attitude and spirit.

They adopted themes from Indian life and situation such as folk-belief, rituals, corruption in socio-political life, miseries of life of the downtrodden and natural calamities. The poetry of Ezekiel, Parthsarathy, K.N. Daruwalla, Adil Jussawalla and Pritish Nandy is replete with picturesque descriptions of contemporary Indian life. These poets were chiefly concerned with the realities of life on which they focus in their verses. Ezekiel, Shiv K. Kumar, Daruwalla and Adil Jussawalla portray the plight of beggars, rickshaw-pullers, vagrants, slum dwellers, prostitutes, child widows and so on with compassion and sympathy. The evils of city life are depicted by Ezekiel, Daruwalla, Jussawalla and Nandy. In contrast to these poets, the Aurobindonians were not at all concerned with the realities of socio-economic problems of India. Their Indian sensibility manifested itself in their adherence to the Vedic and Upanishadic tradition of spiritualism and mysticism. K.S.R Iyengar observes "All modern Indian poetry including Indian English poetry is sustained by the living waters of our racial tradition, the Veda, the Upanishad, the Ramayan, the Mahabharat, the stream of Vaishnava or Shaiva devotional Poetry."[2]

The Aurobindonians also revived English romanticism and romanticized their conception of verses in their poetry. They conceived themes for their poetry by exercising their romantic sensibility and hence their themes are imaginary, visionary, dreamy and meditative. This kind of unrealistic poetry appealed to the Aurobindonians but embittered the taste of the post-Aurobindoninans, who crusaded against that tradition and discarded verses of Aurobindonian flavour. They eschewed elements of romanticism and metaphysical speculation in order to make their poetry a vehicle of social service and reform. S.C. Harrex comments "the new poetry was new because it abhorred the old conventional jargons, sociological as well as literary and rejected romantic or mythic generalizations that deflected the attention from every day realities.[3]

The new poets started writing poetry in the new modernist tradition reposing faith in a vital language, in the value of concreteness, and in the full-time nature of the poet's vocation. They opposed all forms of propaganda, imitation and romanticism and finally asserted their faith in a private voice. The post-Aurobindonians produced a new kind of poetry characterized by surrealism, colloquialism, new idiom and new diction. Thus, Indian poetry in English took a new direction and dimension in the hands of the new poets. Kamala Das writes her poem "An Introduction" in a colloquial manner:

> ...It voices my joys, my longings, my
> Hopes, and it is useful to me as cawing
> Is to crows or roaring to the lions, it
> Is human speech, the speech of the mind that is
> Here and not there.[4]

The Aurobindonians were complacent in their world of myths and legends and gods and goddesses. In the light of these themes of spiritual interest they explored the deeper levels of human mind, truth of life and death enshrouded in the mist of mystery. These themes of myths and mystical experiences had a deep fascination and appeal to them. The post-Aurobindonians on the other hand were psychologically pre-occupied with their self-scrutiny and self-introspection. It is pertinent here to refer—to M.K. Naik's views about Indian literature of the post-independence period "The era of hope, aspiration and certitude was gone: an age of merciless self-scrutiny, questioning and ironic exposure commenced."[5] Among the post-Aurobindonians, there are poets like Ezekiel, Parthasarathy, Dom Moraes, Ramanujan, A.K. Mehrotra and Kamala Das who are well known for externalization of their inwardness. They do not take delight in philosophical speculation about life and death but they are psychologically obsessed in the discovery of their own cultural heritage and roots. The other themes of psychological significance are a sense of alienation, loneliness, nostalgia and exile that impart a distinct identity to the new poetry. The post-Aurobindonians resorted to nostalgic reminiscences and dreamy experiences for a kind of pleasure whereas the Aurobindonian remained engrossed in philosophical contemplation for ecstatic experiences. The post-Aurobindonians disdained the quality and excellence of the Aurobindonian poetry on the ground of exuberance of romanticism and mysticism and resolved to bring this trend of writing to an end. With this objective in view they publicly proclaimed their break with the past with the slogan that "the phase of Indo-Anglian romanticism ended with Sarojini Naidu".[6]

The new modernist poets have a tendency to exploit their own self and personality in poetry for which it becomes a vehicle of autobiographical reflection of the poet's personal experiences. From this viewpoint of use of self, the new poets echo the British poets who have written poetry about their own experiences. Parthasarathy's "Rough Passage," Ezekiel's

"Events and Enterprise", "Night of the Scorpion", Ramanujan's "Small Scale Reflections on a Great House", "Love Poem for a Wife", and Kamala Das's "My Grand Mother's House", "Jaisurya", "Hot Noon at Malbar", etc. are the poems of autobiographical nature. Unlike these new poets the Aurobindonians were far away from exploitation of their self. Their poetry is bereft of any self-revelation or autobiographical reflection. They on the other hand luxuriated in the versification of mystical lyrics but the post-Aurobindonians dismissed such themes based upon these elements. They adopted contemporary social issues of universal interest. M.K. Naik comments "It is strange that certain Indian critics who reverently genuflect before *The Wreck of Deutsland*, *Ash Wednesday* and *The Four Quartets* should turn up their noses at these mystical lyrics."[7]

Another feature of poetry is the theme of love. Both the groups of poets have written poems of love but in the conception and treatment of love they differ entirely from each other. Ezekiel, Kamala Das, Shiv K. Kumar, Pritish Nandy, Daruwalla and Mahapatra have written poems on love, mostly in earthly or psychological terms. In contrast to this kind of erotic love, the Aurobindonians conceived of celestial love of immortal character. The love between Urvasie and Pururavus, Chitrangada and Urjoon, Savitri and Satyavan transcends the boundary of vulnerability, inconsistency and transience. Their love assumes spiritual significance and attains fulfilment. The lover conquers death by love. They never experience any kind of frustration, dejection and anguish in love as Keats, Yeats and Kamala Das had felt in their real life. The lovers in the poetry of the Aurobindonians sublimate their love by virtue of their fidelity, intensity and consistency. The disciples of Sri Aurobindo treated love on a higher spiritual plane. They also deal with mystical love between Man and God and Man and Nature.

In writing these love poems the Aurobindonians have followed the Vedic tradition that treats physical love as sinful and as an impediment on the path of a possible relationship between Man and God. Indian mythology is a storehouse of tales of mythical love. It is out of this repertoire of stories of love that the Aurobindonians have borrowed themes for their love poetry. Whereas the Aurobindonians were inspired by a cult of beauty, lyrical passion and intensity of emotion, the post-Aurobindonians were imbued with a new spirit of creativity, innovation, experiment and novelty. David Mc Cutchion remarks "the poets of fifties were fresh, inventive and individual".[8]

The former group of poets was writing lyrical verse, traditional narrative poetry and poetic drama but the latter group was pre-occupied with free verse and prose poems. Nandy is pre-eminently known for his prose poems, which constituted a new breakthrough in Indian poetry in English. The Aurobindonians considered poetry a vehicle of spirit and emotional exuberance. It served as a communication between Man and God. Unlike the former, the post-Aurobindonians treat poetry as a medium of manifestation of all creative urges. Modern poets embody in their verses new areas of thoughts and philosophy such as Darwinism, Marxism, Buddhism, Gandhism, Feminism, existentialism, positivism and Freudian psychology. The new poets' vision of life is coloured by humanism and irony but the Aurobindonians perceive life spiritually, mystically and symbolically.

In respect of versification the Aurobindonians continued to write in the Miltonic and Keatsian tradition. They used similes, images, symbols, meters, blank verse and vocabulary provided by these British poets. The poetic diction of Sri Aurobindo was interlarded with Miltonic Latinized expressions. His disciples too followed his footsteps in the versification of poetry of this convention. K.D. Sethna, N.K. Gupta, D.K. Roy, Romen and other Aurobindonians wrote exactly or tried to write exactly like their master. They were trained in the art and technique of writing by Sri Aurobindo himself. The poems, written by K.D. Sethna were corrected by him. The corrected scripts give evidence of this training imparted by the master. They all cultivated an elevated style of writing poetry.

Unlike them, the post-Aurobindonians drew inspiration from P. Lal to write a new kind of poetry in accordance with the canons of versification laid down in the Kavita Manifesto (1959). These poets explored new innovative techniques of expression and innovated their own art and artifice in order to assert their own identity and they used the colloquial style and idioms to give vent to their Indian sentiments and sensibility. Their poetry became an expression of their private voices. Satire and irony are salient features of the post-Aurobindonian poetry. Irony is noticed for example in Ezekiel's "Afternoon poem", "The Egoist's Prayers" and "Theological". In Shiv K. Kumar's "In my Co-Respondent" and

"Pilgrimage", we perceive an implicit irony. Similarly Daruwalla uses irony in the poem "Fire-Hymn".

Symbolism is used by the new modernist under the influence of the French poets and British poets like Eliot, Yeats and Wyndham and Lewis. H.M. William remarks "In many cases the new poetry was generated by the acceptance of a new set of influences. In place English and Indian Romantic poets came the influence of the British poets or the modernist poets, who echo Yeats, Eliot and Pound."[9]

In Ezekiel's poems, "Crow", "Night of the Scorpion" and "Enterprise", the underlying meaning of the poems can be inferred symbolically. To Ezekiel, the crow is a symbol of evil and sin. Likewise, the scorpion in the "Night of the Scorpion" suggests the pervading evils. These symbols sometimes rendered poetry obscure and obfuscate the meaning. The poetry of A.K. Mehrotra, Mahapatra and Kolatkar is often called the poetry of obscurity and ambiguity from this viewpoint. The post-Aurobindonians used images in poetry. Women, body of women, city and nature are recurring images, which assume symbolic overtones in their verses. Unlike these poets, the Aurobindonians used the traditional symbols to avoid confusion and vagueness. They used various elements of nature as symbols to enrich poetry.

The Aurobindonians imbibed the influences of Milton, Wordsworth, Keats and Tennyson and assimilated them to their own Indian sensibility. The post-Aurobindonians on the other hand criticized the Aurobindonians as imitators on this ground of such absorption of Western influences. Ironically, they forgot that they themselves had written poetry under the influence of the British and Americans poets, like Hopkins, Yeats, Eliot, Pound, Wyndham, Lewis and Allen Tate. In the words of M.K. Naik "They (two groups of poets pre- and post-poets) have merely exchanged the king Log of Milton, Shelley and Tennyson for the king Stork of Pound, Eliot and Yeats. It is specially Eliot, who is too much with these poets, for poetry for them seems to be almost synonymous with Eliotry". (10)

The post-Aurobindonians revolted with an anti-Aurobindonian spirit against the persistence of old tradition of writing romantic and mystical lyrics and professed their superiority to the Aurobindonians for their new kind of surrealistic and representative forms of poetry woven in a new thread of language. Nevertheless they reckoned their Aurobindonian predecessors as versatile poets in view of latter's exquisiteness of versification Iyengar states "Although the anti-Aurobindonians look upon Sri Aurobindo as their Milton and Tagore and Sarojini Naidu as romantic singing birds yet they waged a war against them through criticism."[11]

Despite the inception and predominance of new tradition of poetry, there are poets like B.B. Paymaster and Adil K. Sette, who continue to write verses in the well-established Aurobindonian tradition. In the case of poets like Kamala Das, we find a unique blend of the physical as well as the spiritual aspects of life. She writes about her personal physical love and aspires for its spiritual transcendence. She desires to elevate and sublimate her love to the level of mythical love of Radha and Krishna.

There are also poets among the post-Aurobindonians, who instead of siding with any of these two groups stand poised between them. Mokashi Punekar and R.Y. Deshpande are modernist poets, who steer a middle course and oscillate between the Aurobindonians and post-Aurobindonians, between traditionalists and the new modernists and between the sentimentalists and the intellectualists. Mokashi Punekar voices his predicament in the poem "The Rejected Race". He writes:

> "We poets are race
>
> Rejected by two worlds"

The contrastive study of the poetical features and traditions of the Aurobindonians and the post-Aurobindonians drives us to a conclusion that these two groups of poets stand irreconcilable because they march uncompromisingly along two different paths of poetry that run in opposite directions. The former followed the path of the Vedic and Upanishadic tradition in poetry and the latter group proceeded along the new path of modernism to post-modernism. Since their directions are different without any meeting point, the Aurobindonians and the post-Aurobindonians can never be reconciled at any point of concordance or agreement in the line of Indian English poetry.

Thus, both groups of poets sustain their own tradition of versification and traverse along their respective paths pioneered by their masters. At the end we reassert in unequivocal terms the existence of two traditions, the Aurobindonian and the post-Aurobindonian, which in other terms are traditionalism and modernism or new symbolism and new modernism. Although these traditions have conflicting groups of poets in respect of differences in aesthetics of poetry and ideology yet both have generated talented and versatile poets and produced rich poetical works which are reckoned as the literary monuments of world literature.

Notes and References

1. M.K. Naik, *Dimension of Indian English Literature*. New Delhi: Sterling Publications, 1984, 9.
2. K.S.R. Iyengar, *Indian Writing in English*. New Delhi: Sterling Publications, 1983, 642.
3. S.C. Harrex. "Small Scale Reflection on Indian English Language Poetry." *The Journal of Indian Writing in English*, Vol. 8, 1980: 137-66.
4. Kamala Das. *An Introduction: The Playhouse and Other Poems*. Delhi: Orient Longman, 1973: 12-14.
5. M.K. Naik, *Perspectives on Indian Poetry in English*. New Delhi: Abhinaba Publications, 1984.
6. P. Lal, *Modern Indian Poetry in English: An Anthology and a Credo* (ed.). Calcutta: Writers Workshop, 1969.
7. M.K. Naik, *The Humanities Review*, Vol. 4: 26.
8. David McCutchion, *Indian Writing in English*. Calcutta: Writers Workshop, 1969.
9. H.M. Witliam, *Indo-Anglian Literature 1800-1970: A Survey*. New Delhi: Orienting Man, 1976.
10. M.K. Naik, *Aspects of Indian Writing in English*. New Delhi: Macmillan, 1979: 42.
11. K.S.R. Iyengar, *Indian Writing in English*. Delhi: Sterling Publications, 1984: 653.

□

Witnessing England: T.N. Mukharji's *A Visit to Europe*

Amrita Satapathy

Colonial feudalism had paved the way for commercial travel, giving a sense of restrained mobility to the colonized. Besides documenting and mapping, travel became essentially a way of counteracting the embroidered idea of nationhood and exposing, "multiple sites of contestation and cooperation as well as inconsistencies and contradictions among both Britons and Indians" (Fisher 2004: 13). Interestingly, most Indians who travelled belonged to the educated elite and were of the firm belief that "Anglicization, democracy, and social reform are the paths to progress" (Fisher 2004: 14). They went on a mission to closely study developed societies and find the cure for the social ills afflicting British India. The time had come for advertising an authentic idea of England. After all London was "the center of empire, of political, commercial, and cultural power: 'the capital of the human race'" (Brigitte Bailey 1995: 201). As the twin notions of nationhood and citizenship were developing, so the sense of "becoming" was being unconsciously reinforced among travellers. As Antoinette Burton claims that when Indians went to the "heart of the Empire", they not only saw themselves as "Colonial subjects" but also "worked to remake that very category by reappropriating the imperial gaze" (Peering Back 205).[1] Educated and enlightened colonial subjects like Trailokyanath Mukharji who went to England, saw the country as a way to redeem themselves from the "subject-citizen" tag. Mukharji's travelography is a social commentary on the culturally inept English and their fascination with the East, "...the very imbibing of the Euroimperial notions of travel enabled the colonized to often deploy them in ways that would crucially challenge the Western claim to indisputable cultural superiority" (Sen 7-8).

A Visit to Europe is a manifesto on how travel can become an information gathering and edifying endeavour. It vindicates Bankim

Chandra Chatterjee appraisal of Romesh Chandra Dutta's *Three Years in Europe* which beautifully articulates the idea of England:

> As a result of our English education we have come to know a great deal about England from English books and we have also seen many Englishmen in our country. Still our knowledge of England is as scanty as that of a blind man who tried to form an idea of the elephant simply by touching it. When we read English books written by Englishmen and the England painted by them is typically an Englishman's view of England. What England will look through our Indian eyes we are unable to see in English publications.[2]

It has all the elements by which the modern Indian traveller's Self projects itself in contradiction to its European Other—"an aestheticized conception of nature, a critical attitude towards industrial culture, a nostalgic longing for the past and so on..." (Sen 8). It is symbolic of the transformations that travel memoirs were undergoing by directing their gaze on "reflecting the shifting aesthetic and cultural fashions of the day, as well as the power inequalities that lie between East and West, the history of empire, and the gendered spaces of home and abroad" (Hooper and Youngs 2004: 3-4). Mukharji throws a new light on how the East/easterners claimed their agency—by noting their impressions, observations, and detailing their excursions in the distant land of England: "Since much of the period's travel literature is the direct product of colonial and imperialist enterprises, encounters with ideological otherness are a central preoccupation of most travel writers of the period" (Scott. D. Juall 2008: 1-4).

Mukharji's account of his visit is by a native who not only has a good understanding of his own country but also of Europe and European life. The travelogue is not only an exhaustive study but also an expose on the Empire. Thus,

> The observations and reflections of such a traveler ought to be of interest alike to the Hindu and the European. The Hindu cannot fail to regard the account as something like a revelation; and the European will learn to see himself as others see him. (1889 xi)

Mukharji comes across as a broad-minded and unprejudiced traveler. He deftly assumes the garb of the *flâneur*—the itinerant observer of city and contemporary life. For him the visit becomes an eye-opening experience. He is not the effeminate Bengali[3]—lethargic, bookish, and staid and unruly here. Rather he comes across as very alert and sagacious individual who is liberal minded and interactive. His tone is at once condescending and instructive and he writes with an edifying purpose—"...the whole nation is suffering from a mental aberration which my country-men fondly call *intense religiousness*" (39) and that is what makes him an ideal spokesperson and interpreter for the people of colonial India. Through his travelogue he attempts to illuminate British society and its metropolitan culture, and records his astute observations by mincing no words,

> The manners of an English man, however, undergo some change when he is outside his own country, whether it be in France, Germany or Italy. Outside his own country, he is proud, somewhat disdainful, and not too anxious to conceal in his breast that opinion which every nation in the world entertains—that all other nations are inferior to itself. Not only with him, but as a rule with every man, this feeling of superiority is intensified when he finds himself amongst a people manifestly and vastly inferior to his own. He finds it impossible, for instance, to be on equal terms with a people whose low organization permitted their being reduced from time immemorial to the position of cattle, and who has been rescued from this position solely by his clemency. That portion of the human race which gave such a signal proof of its low organization was always distinguished by the colour of its skin; and the universal decadence of all coloured races in the present cycle has in the eyes of the Europeans effaced all nicety of distinction among them, has divided the human race by one broad line into two main classes—the white and the coloured.... (117-18)

'First Impressions' gives us a vivid idea of London. Nowhere do we get the impression that first time traveler Mukharji is in unfamiliar terrain. It is as if he has been there already and the journey is just a confirmation to his imaginings. As Bhaskar Mukhopadhyay asserts:

> "For these colonial tourists, travel to England was not so much a journey into the unknown as a confirmation of what was already known about England thanks to 'print capitalism' and 'travel capitalism.'[4] Our travelers were not on the lookout for the marvelous and the unknown—their gaze constantly scrutinized whether the real England measured up to their hyperreal image of England."[5] The

sights and sounds of London city "combine to create a grandeur of busy life which must be seen to be fully realized." (1889: 34)

Like Krisnabhabini Das who writes in her *Englandey Bangamahila* that "The English were advertisement maniacs" (Sen 79). Trailokyanath too directs his critical eye towards the commodifying trend gaining momentum in capitalist Europe, "The best of everything is here offered for sale at the cheapest price, its merit being often illustrated with pictures of fantastic designs" (34). He is quick to note the estrangement with reality when it comes to the perception of other cultures even in advertisements. So much so that "the black races need no longer have the fear of being eaten up by white men for the sake of their complexion, for a single application of Mr. Pears' Soap will whiten the blackest of black faces" (35). According to Mukharji, London is the "City…the centre of the earth, the heart which supplies the life-blood to the commerce of the world, and sends forth the impulse by force". It is "microcosm of the world" (1889: 40). So he isn't very judgmental towards the English's business acumen, as far as advertising is concerned. It was an employment generating tool—"Besides printers, engravers, sandwich boys and others in the regular line, there are agents who undertake to do this work for merchants and manufacturers; then it has also given rise to inventors of new paints, new types, new boards and new machines, used solely for this purpose" (35).

T.N. Mukharji's book heralds the "emergence of a new intellectual political conscience" (Said 1994: xxvii), where interactions with the West led to the formation of cultures that were not homogenous but heterogenous; hybrid and not stagnated; monolithic and yet varied in more ways than one. People were able to perceive that there is no one culture but a plurality of cultures. There is not one geographical domain, but numerous. The passage from one continent to another was not just confined to an aesthetic exploration; rather it was one of historical investigation. The context of *The Colonial and Indian Exhibition* which opens on 4 May 1886 makes this obvious. Though the display of the wonders of the East is humiliating for the curator he goes on to say, "We were interesting beings in the eyes of the Londoners, who had oftener opportunities of seeing their fellow subjects from the far East" (1889: 102) and were treated as gentlemen would treat gentlemen; "A fellow feeling existed between the Anglo-Indians and ourselves as if they were our countrymen in that strange land…however slight it might be, and their power and superiority over us" (1889: 106). He says with a touch a bitter irony,

> Such alas! Is the will of the nation at the present moment, the effect of a reaction and of the praise bestowed by generous westerners on everything that is Hindu. A more effective method could not be devised to ruin a highly sensitive and proud people laboring under physical and mental infirmities and demoralized by centuries of foreign domination. (1889: 77)

Literate and cultured gentlemen and ladies honour the visitors "as the representatives of the most ancient nation now existing on the face of the earth" (1889: 101). But more often than not—"They were as much astonished to see the Indians produce works of art with the aid of crude apparatus they themselves had discarded long ago, as Hindu would be to see a chimpanzee officiating as a priest in a funeral ceremony and reading out Sanskrit texts from a palm leaf spread before him" (99). Though, on the personal front Mukharji, has mixed experiences as a 'subject' under the colonial rule and in his own words he is at one time a foreigner, a subject, a blackie, an honoured guest, an Indian, a Hindu; yet "He is no foreigner!. He is a British subject as you and I" (1889: 108), and "He is Trailokya Nath Mukharji, dark-skinned Hindu representing the English to those they have subjugated and to themselves" (Childers 300).

Traveling to London made Mukharji aware of his "native" status and it is, he realizes imperative that Indians overcame this socio-political tag- "We are all 'natives' now—We poor Indians, the aborigines of Australia and the South Sea Islands, the Negroes, the Kaffirs, the Hottentots and other races of Africa. The Egyptians have lately become 'natives'. The Chinese, the Japanese, the Persians and the Turks are not 'natives'" (1889: 132). Though he is treated as a guest, as mentioned earlier, and is considered a part of the Empire, he still cannot resist the tag. It clings to him unconsciously. And the Colonial Exhibition in more ways than one highlights this fact:

> In England a French, German or Italian is a "foreigner", an Indian or an African is a "native". Colour has much to do with the making of a "native", but as Harris of "Uncle Tom's Cabin" found to his cost, human beings of the "native" kind are not always distinguished by colour. Fair or dark, we in India are all "natives". (1889: 132)

Although the Queen's Proclamation of 1885 declared "…Our subjects, of whatever Race, or Creed; be freely and impartially admitted to Offices in Our Service, the Duties of which they may be qualified, by their education, ability, and integrity, duly to observe". Joseph Chamberlain makes this catachrestic proclamation evident when he puts forth the view, "But we ask you also to bear in mind the traditions of the Empire which make no distinction in favour of, or against race or colour", Mukharji is emotionally invested enough to gauge the true nature of the colonizer-colonized relationship, and in consequence the subject-citizen divide, when he points out, "We were pierced through and through by stares from eyes of all colours—green, gray, blue, black—and every movement and act of ours, walking, sitting, eating, reading, received its full share of "O, I, never!" (99-100). He is very aware of how the colonial is looked at in the land of the whites and his scrutiny throws light on "the limits of the imperial imagination: the aspect of colonialism that accounts for those popular perceptions of the other that, regardless of accuracy, predominate and contribute to shared comprehensions of the empire and those who 'out there' in it" (Peering Back 206). Interestingly, Mukharji is not just the native here; he is "one of those inhabiting the places the traveller travelled to see".[6] The traveller in him is discerning and flexible to comprehend other's view about him. He moves in unrestrained ways as an imperial citizen among the whites.

According to Mukharji, "In India we see very little of the English people. Neither do we know them nor do they know us. So in England we found ourselves entirely among strangers of whom practically we knew nothing except the language" (1889, 118-19). He goes on to say on a jocular note, that the peculiarity of the Englishman's behaviour in his country and in India is because "A fish *out of* water is not exactly the fish *in* water"; for the Englishman India is an un-navigable but lucrative colony where he assumes a larger than life stature and behaves so. Through his description of the English, Mukharji is able to challenge imperial subjection, much like Mirza Abu Taleb who documented his own views on the English in his "Travels of Mirza Abu Taleb" around 1799-1803. Simonti Sen writes,

> From Abu Taleb the readers also got a list of virtues and vices of the English people. While in fairness to them he referred to qualities such as a sense of respect for their superiors, their obedience to law, their desire for philanthropy and hospitality, he provided

> lengthier account of their vices, namely lack of faith in religion, pride and insolence, passion for money, desire for ease and dislike for exertion...discourteous manners, irritability of temper, whiling away of time in pursuit of sensuous pleasures, luxurious manner of living and so on. (42-43)

The fact that Asians could narrate their experiences in their own words and in their own terms, became "a powerful mode of resistance to European cultural domination" (Fisher 2004: 17). Mukharji's travelogue showed that the British and the Empire could be assessed, something that they hadn't faced before. Unlike the English who painted their own versions of the images of India, Indians were very concrete and true to their portrayals. Mukharji describes with a precision that is almost clinical and scientific. Joseph Childers's comment provides validation for colonial travelogues like *A Visit to Europe*,

> Such acts of self-discovery and reappropriation provide alternative accounts to the English experience of the display of empire during 1886-87. The narratives of these visitors offer us insights into the delicate balance their authors maintained between participating in, even cooperating with, Britain's portrayal of it imperial supremacy to itself, on the one hand, and, on the other, recognizing the power they held over that display by placing a human face upon it. (2007: 205-06).

Mukharji is the highest-ranking South Asian in the Department of Revenue and Agriculture in colonial India. He is also the curator of one of the important collection assigned to the Bengali Economic Museum. He was put in charge of overseeing the arts and manufactures displays and demonstration in the Indian Hall of the Colonial and Indian Exhibition. Though an Indian of profound importance, he still remains a "subject"—an exhibit of sorts, showcasing himself, his nativity, his Indian identity in the heart of the Empire-London. His travelogue not only unravels the mystique of being an Indian from inscrutable India, it also unravels charismatic imperial London for us. It is a classic case of looking at and being looked at. *A Visit to Europe* becomes the discursive point of intersection between the two 'gazes'. Though the book is about the Indian and the Colonial Exhibition, in a way the colonizer English become the spectacle. And the negotiation between two cultures, two minds, and two time frames gives a distinctively different dimension to this diasporic narrative. Mukharji's travelogue not only "accounts of exploration" but also of "colonial conquest and administration" (Thompson 2011: 19). It is modern travel book in the sense that it contains a diversity of matter—ranging from seen and felt experiences to new encounters with new people and culture and commentaries on them. The visitors from India learn to navigate and learn the social ways of England—"We were too green to note the intensity of caste and political prejudices in England." They admit albeit candidly "To us all Britishers (including the Irish) were alike, high or low, conservative or radical." Class consciousness was a prominent feature in London high society, "We knew not that friendliness for the low was a sin against the high, sympathy for the radical an offence against the conservative" (1889: 140). Europe in the words of Mukharji, is suffering from a state of "self-abnegation" (1889: 299). It is at this juncture that he reincarnates into the veritable Occidental observer who successfully paints a wordy picture of a politically monotheistic England.

Though the travelogue lacks mobility, in the sense the reader doesn't get to travel along with the traveller, Mukharji is able to capture the pacy spirit of a fin de siècle[7] London that was evolving from a materialist, rationalist, bourgeois society and championing the cause of liberal democracy on home turf, but was, paradoxically, advocating unconstructive social determinants in its colonies. As Joseph Childers posits, "…Mukharji's commentary at once both lauds and lampoons those characteristics that are instantly recognizable as the "essence" of English national identity at the end of the nineteenth century…" (Childers 299). Besides through his travel narrative he was able to showcase India as the country it is. Mukharji challenges the widely circulating imperialistic and discrepant images of the East. Since the entire idea of undertaking a voyage was essentially an imperialistic exercise, where notions about culture and identity were "clarified, reinforced, criticized or rejected".[8]

It brings to the fore, what Trailokyanath himself says, "the tyrannical sway of fashion" (159). He is impressed yet appalled by the Westerner's fetish for fashion and therein he suggests lies the seed of decadence. There is a hint of sarcasm when he says, "The subject of fashion often set me wondering. It impressed me with the thought that human race is a race of slaves…. True that the Western world is preparing to bring about a great social cataclysm but what of that?" (159). Like Vivekananda who in his book *Prachyo O Paschatya* condemns European frivolity and diagnoses a superficiality and artificiality that underlies the very basis of

European hegemony—the excesses of Western epistemology, Mukharji too sees this as a deluge that comes with "a new set of well furbished fetters, beautiful to look at in their fresh state and quite effective to enchain humanity for the rest of the epoch" (159). Thus a travel book like *A Visit to Europe*, becomes in Mary Campbell's words, "a kind of witness" that is "generically aimed at the truth" (15). In spite of that it has a marked uncertainty about it; sometimes one is baffled by the author's sense of fealty—is it to his motherland or to the Empire. The answer lies "uncertainties about their relations to the discourses of empire; uncertainties that constrain their subjectivities both in England and in their own lands (Childers 206).

Seventeenth century saw the movement of diplomats, merchants, explorers, colonizers, scientists and curators. This was the age which saw the development of travel writing from romantic escapades and adventure to mercantile capitalism. The travel to England shows Mukharji as a moderate citizen of imperial Raj, someone who navigates within the confines of a realist narrative chronotope. Mukharji being a Brahmin, a man belonging to the highest caste in India, and literate, someone who could engage with the Empire in their tongue and who could navigate comfortably in their society, remains unaffected. "We care very little whether they call us "natives" or "niggers". Our ambition should always be higher. It is to make the nation rich, whole humanity powerful, comfortable and happy" (1889: 134). He aims through his narrative to show both India and England through the lens of imperial citizenship. Both nations had been imagined by each other until now. Incidentally if one reads carefully Mukharji's travelogue, England also seems like a strange land, providing an escape to the exotic akin to what lands in the east had once upon a time been. Mukharji appears a little ambivalent in the narrative, nevertheless it reinforces his egalitarian and emancipatory views regarding his motherland. *A Visit to Europe* is an engagement with experiences observed and natural satisfaction of curiosity about another culture. It presents a multidimensional view of two disparate yet distinct cultures. As Paul Fussel, argues a travelogue is not a work of fiction because of its claim on 'literary validity' and its 'constant reference to actuality'; rather as Carl Thompson puts it, it is a representation of a journey, and of events on that journey *that really took place*[9] (2011: 15).

Notes

1. Exhibitions and festivals organized in England by the colonies in 1886 and 1887 manifested into re-discovery and re-appropriation from the point of view of the colonial visitors. Curators like Mukharji maintained a delicate and managed a fragile balance between participating and cooperating with the imperial supremacy and at the same time offering their personal, critical and colonial insights into metropolitan London; see Eds. James Buzard, Joseph W. Childers, Eileen Gilooly, *Victorian Prism* 203-15.
2. *Bangadarshan*, Bankim Chandra Chatterjee February-March 1873. Repr., Calcutta: Reflect Publishers, 1974.
3. Mrinalini Sinha in her book *Colonial Masculinity: The "Manly Englishman"* and the "Effeminate" Bengali in the Late nineteenth century mentions that the middle class, English-educated Bengali was perceived by the British as "the stock figure of the 'weak-kneed, effeminate, effete Bengalee'…" (104). For further reference see *Colonial Masculinity: The "Manly Englishman"* and the "Effeminate" Bengali in the Late Nineteenth Century. By Mrinalini Sinha. Manchester: Manchester University Press, 1995.
4. The term 'travel capitalism' has been borrowed from the essay by Jozsef Borocz, *Travel-Capitalism: The Structure of Europe and the Advent of the Tourist*, Comparative Studies in Society and History, Vol. 34, No. 4 (Oct. 1992), 708-41, Cambridge University.
5. In his essay, *Writing Home, Writing Travel: The Poetics and Politics of Dwelling in Bengali Modernity*, Comparative Studies in Society and History, Vol. 44, No. 2 (Apr. 2002), Cambridge University, Bhaskar Mukhopadhyay, uses the term 'hyperreal' in the sense that most colonized Indians who visited England suffered from a clash of visualization between the 'imagined', virtual and bookish/fictional idea of England and the real, seen and experienced idea of England.
6. Elizabeth A. Bohls and Ian Duncan, *Travel Writing* 1700-1830: *An Anthology*, xvi.
7. *The Encyclopedia Britannica* defines the word 'fin de siècle' as (French: "end of the century") of, relating to, characteristic of, or resembling the late 19th-century literary and artistic climate of sophistication, escapism, extreme aestheticism, world-weariness, and fashionable despair. Antoinette Burton in her article *Making a Spectacle of Empire: Indian Travelers in Fin-de-Siècle London* talks about how in the 19th century a lot of travel writings evolved from the Indian subcontinent and how the travelers, bearing the tag of 'colonised' subjects viewed and reviewed the Imperial nation in their own terms. Indian travelers saw an England that was evolving from a colonizing agency to a nation undergoing tumultuous changes socially,

politically, religiously, economically and most importantly in spirit from cosmopolitan to decadent.

8. Edward Said, *Culture and Imperialism*, 9.
9. Carl Thompson, *Travel Writing*, 15.

Works Cited

Banerjee, Sukanya. 2010. *Becoming Imperial Citizens: Indians in Late-Victorian Empire*: Durham and London: Duke University Press.

Brigitte, Bailey. June, 1995. *Travel Writing and the Metropolis: James, London, and English Hours*, American Literature, Vol. 67, (2): 201-32, Duke University Press. doi: http://www.jstor.org/stable/2927787

Boehmer, Elleke. 1995. *Colonial & Post-Colonial Literature*, OUP.

Bohls A. Elizabeth and Duncan Ian. eds. 2005. *Travel Writing 1700-1830: An Anthology*, OUP.

Borocz, Jozsef. Oct. 1992. *Travel-Capitalism: The Structure of Europe and the Advent of the Tourist, Comparative Studies in Society and History*, Vol. 34, (4): 708-41, Cambridge University. doi: http://www.jstor.org/stable/179354

Burton, Antoinette Autumn, 1996. *Making a Spectacle of Empire: Indian Travelers in Fin-de-Siècle London. History Workshop Journal*, No. 42: 126-46. Oxford University Press. doi: http://www.jstor.org/stable/4289470

Childers, Joseph, W. 2007. "Peering Back", Part Four in *Victorian Prism: Refractions of the Crystal Palace*, edited by Buzard, James, Childers, Joseph W, Gilooly, Eileen. 203-15.

Charlottesville and London: University of Virginia Press.

Codell, Julie, F. March 2007. *Reversing the Grand Tour: Guest Discourse in Indian Travel Narratives. Huntington Library Quarterly*, Vol. 70(1): 173-89, University of California Press, doi: http://www.jstor.org/stable/10.1525/hlq.2007.70.1.173?origin=JSTOR-pdf

Davin, Anna. 1978. *Imperialism and Motherhood. History Workshop*, No. 5 (Spring, 1978): 9-65. Oxford University Press. doi: http://www.jstor.org/stable/4288158

Fisher, Michael H. 2004. *Counterflows to Colonialism: Indian Travelers and Settlers in Britain from 1600-1857*. New Delhi: Permanent Black.

Fisher, Michael H. March, 2007. *From India to England and Back: Early Indian Travel Narratives for Indian Readers. Huntington Library Quarterly*, Vol. 70, (1). University of California Press doi. http://www.jstor.org/stable/4289470

Hooper, Glen and Youngs Tim. eds. 2004. *Perspectives on Travel Writings*. England: Ashgate Publishing Limited.

Hulme, Peter and Youngs, Tim. eds. 2011. *Cambridge Companion to Travel Writing*. UK: Cambridge University Press.

Juall, Scott D. 2008. *(Re)writing Self and Other in Early Modern French Travel Literature*. L'Esprit Créateur, Vol. 48(1): 1-4.

Mukharji, T.N. 1889. *A Visit to Europe*. British Library: Historical Print Editions.

Mukhopadhyay, Bhaskar. Apr. 2002. *Writing Home, Writing Travel: The Poetics and Politics of Dwelling in Bengali Modernity, Comparative Studies in Society and History*, Vol. 44, No. 2, 293. Cambridge University, URL: http://www.jstor.org/stable/3879448

Said Edward. 1994. *Culture and Imperialism*. Random House.

Said, Edward. 2001. *Orientalism*. India: Penguin Books India.

Sen, Simonti. 2005. *Travels to Europe: Self and Other in Bengali Narratives 1870-1910*. London, UK: Sangam Books Limited.

Thompson, Carl. 2011. *Travel Writing, The New Critical Idiom*. Abingdon, Oxford: Routledge.

Tosh, John. 1994. *What Should Historians Do with Masculinity? Reflections on Nineteenth-Century Britain. History Workshop*, No. 38: 179-202. Oxford University Press. doi: http://www.jstor.org/stable/4289324?origin=JSTOR-pdf

Windholz, M. Anne. Summer, 1999-Summer, 2000. *An Emigrant and a Gentleman: Imperial Masculinity, British Magazines, and the Colony That Got Away*. Victorian Studies, Vol. 42, No. 4: 631-58. Indian University Press. doi: http://www.jstor.org/stable/3829990?origin=JSTOR-pdf

Yule, Henry and Burnell, A.C. 2008. *The Concise Hobson-Jobson*: *An Anglo-Indian Dictionary*.

Wordsworth Reference Series. London: Wordsworth Editions.

Youngs, Tim. ed. 2006. *Travel Writing in the Nineteenth Century*: *Filling the Blank Spaces*. UK: Anthem Press.

□